Curt has an incredible gift for weaving together the wisdom and truth of God's Word with the wisdom and truth of science in a profoundly unique way. Reading his words gives you the sense that you're sitting with a friend who cares deeply, has an incredibly deep well of experience to draw from, is willing to be honest and vulnerable about his own journey, and all the while just happens to be a brilliant doctor of the mind, body, and soul. I'm a true fan of Curt's heart and his work, and I have no doubt that this book will be a great source of hope and help in the deepest places for everyone who reads it.

STEVEN CURTIS CHAPMAN, GRAMMY® Award-winning singer-songwriter

There's a reality that none of us willingly want to face—that our lives will inevitably include suffering. And while the hardest part is to hold that truth, in *The Deepest Place* Curt offers us stories and strategies to navigate it all with grace, grit, and the acceptance of grief. On the other side of these words is lasting hope. I pray you read them. You deserve it.

TONI COLLIER, hope coach, speaker, podcast host, and author of *Brave Enough to Be Broken*

With his formidable intellect and compassionate heart, Curt Thompson draws from Scripture, neurobiology, and inspiring stories to help people advance on the path from suffering to hope and redemption. This is a spiritual formation *tour de force* for anyone ready to look life's inescapable pain in the eye and make something better of it. A must-read.

IAN MORGAN CRON, bestselling author of *The Story of You*

Curt continues to be one of our most winsome and wise teachers and one of our most beloved friends. This stunning new guidebook offers a shimmering light at the end of all our darkest tunnels, gently drawing us through the pain toward something gloriously hopeful together.

KATHERINE AND JAY WOLF, authors of *Hope Heals*, *Suffer Strong*, and *Treasures in the Dark*

Curt Thompson has the prophetic audacity to suggest that the agonies you have suffered in life can be redeemed . . . but the redemption of your pain will require interpersonal relationships. Trauma and pain begin to heal when our stories are witnessed by an empathetic other. In *The Deepest Place*,

Thompson invites you to reimagine how your suffering can be redeemed by engaging your story with others.

ADAM YOUNG. therapist and host of *The Place We Find Ourselves* podcast

Both gentle and compelling, this book invites us to redefine our relationship with suffering, offering us the possibility of building lives of courage marked by resilience. Rather than enduring dizzying lives where we grasp for momentary relief through coping strategies, we now have a way to transform suffering into durable hope.

JESSICA HONEGGER. founder of Noonday Collection, author of *Imperfect Courage*

Curt does it again with *The Deepest Place*. It's brilliant! He guides us along to discover how our lives, our pain, and our joy were meant to intersect the greatest story ever told. Curt pulls us in close and unveils God's deep love and desire for us to more fully experience a life we hardly ever give ourselves permission to pursue. The stories he tells and advice he gives are like a caring, patient friend, helping us self-discover the enormous ways our suffering becomes our greatest strength.

GABE LYONS. president, THINQ Media

All of us suffer, in many ways: in relationships, in families, in work, and in health. And, because suffering is painful, we look for ways to end it, or reduce it. Yet God provides another, deeper, and ultimately better way to deal with suffering. Through Curt Thompson's extensive expertise as a psychiatrist, his knowledge of the Scriptures, and his own vulnerable and warm style, he guides us into a path that helps us engage with suffering, deal with it, embrace that which must be embraced, and transform us to a life of faith, love, and hope. Highly recommended.

JOHN TOWNSEND. PhD, author of the *New York Times* bestselling Boundaries series; founder, Townsend Institute and Townsend Leadership Program

Our world is suffering in a way I've never experienced as a therapist with kids and families for thirty years. It is debilitating. It is isolating. And it certainly feels hopeless at times. We need strong, thoughtful voices reminding us of the promise of redemption. Of the purpose in sharing our stories.

And of the hope that we can experience today through the gospel of Christ. Curt Thompson is one of those voices who points us with biblical wisdom, science-backed evidence, and plentiful grace to that hope.

SISSY GOFF, director of Child & Adolescent Counseling, Daystar Counseling, author of the bestselling *Raising Worry-Free Girls*

Curt Thompson has done it again! No other voice today more skillfully weaves together expertise in psychology, neurobiology, and biblical theology and threads it all together with pastoral sensitivity and graceful writing. Curt brings all of this to bear on the most perplexing aspect of human existence: suffering. The book does not explain away pain with platitudes but tenderly examines human suffering in the raw, especially via stories from Curt's own medical practice. Most importantly, the book takes readers to that deepest place indeed: the path marked out by Jesus and the apostle Paul, where we are invited to go *through* suffering with the hope of God's redemption. It is a path we all must travel—and we are blessed to have Curt as a guide.

CURTIS CHANG, author of *The Anxiety Opportunity*, host of the *Good Faith* podcast, consulting professor, Duke Divinity School, and senior fellow, Fuller Theological Seminary

In *The Deepest Place*, Dr. Curt Thompson brilliantly brings to light the intersecting paths of hope, suffering, and human connection. Intricately woven with strands of faith, interpersonal neurobiology, and the transformative power of relationships, this book compels us to journey toward the full realization of our God-given humanity. It's a call to traverse life's arduous terrain with fortitude, strengthened by the profound and nurturing embrace of others, each steeped in the all-encompassing presence of grace. Curt's work is a gift to so many who are yearning to find a deeper understanding of how our Trinitarian faith informs our embodied humanity.

DR. ALISON COOK, therapist, author of *The Best of You* and *Boundaries for Your Soul*

Among the books written on the subject of suffering, *The Deepest Place* is in an elite class by itself. Thompson's exegesis of Scripture, clinical wisdom, and scientific understanding of interpersonal neurobiology gives readers the widest possible lens to see that suffering is not something to merely endure. Instead, we learn the essential ingredients for deeply embedded hope to form in the places where it is least likely to be experienced. We learn how to be hospitable to the pain and suffering. We learn that, although there are no guarantees of escaping suffering, we have been given an ancient path to suffer differently, a tried-and-true path upon which we discover in our bones that love has us.

MICHAEL JOHN CUSICK, author of *Surfing for God*, CEO at Restoring the Soul

In *The Deepest Place*, Curt Thompson once again guides us into goodness with the hallmark gentleness and acumen we've come to trust in his books. Curt so beautifully translates incredibly complex insights about the human body, soul, and relationships into words that welcome us into wholeness. *The Deepest Place* will pierce your imagination with the possibility that your groans and grief really might be the place you encounter your greatest glory.

K. J. RAMSEY, trauma therapist, author of *The Book of Common Courage* and *The Lord Is My Courage*

In this powerful book, grounded in sacred Scripture, neuroscience, and clinical experience, Curt Thompson teaches us to become hopeful amid human suffering through forming ever-deepening, secure attachment with the hurting parts of our own selves, with one another, and with Jesus. What could be more important?

KIMBERLY MILLER, MTh, LMFT, author of *Boundaries for Your Soul: How to Turn Your Overwhelming Thoughts and Feelings into Your Greatest Allies*

I spent a season of my life living in Southern California and lived through several fires within those years. For months following each fire, we were surrounded by black, scorched earth. But then the rain would come, and the most tender green would emerge. The destructive fire was the *very thing* that made the soil rich for new growth—a picture of God's redemption in the wake of what we thought was ruined. Weaving his wealth of knowledge and experience as a psychiatrist with his careful study of Scripture, Curt shows us that like a fire, our pain can be the very thing that keeps us tethered to the hope of Christ, where our hearts are transformed and new growth can emerge. I read everything Curt writes with anticipation. God has used his work (including this book) in my personal transformation journey. I'm so excited for you to have *The Deepest Place* too . . . it's a gift for us all.

NICOLE ZASOWSKI, marriage and family therapist, author of *What If It's Wonderful?*

CURT THOMPSON, MD

THE
DEEPEST
PLACE

SUFFERING AND THE
FORMATION OF HOPE

ZONDERVAN
BOOKS

ZONDERVAN BOOKS

The Deepest Place
Copyright © 2023 by Curt Thompson, MD

Requests for information should be addressed to:
Zondervan, *3900 Sparks Dr. SE, Grand Rapids, Michigan 49546*

Zondervan titles may be purchased in bulk for educational, business, fundraising, or sales promotional use. For information, please email SpecialMarkets@Zondervan.com.

ISBN 978-0-310-36649-2 (audio)

Library of Congress Cataloging-in-Publication Data

Names: Thompson, Curt, 1962- author.
Title: The deepest place : suffering and the formation of hope / Curt Thompson, MD.
Description: Grand Rapids : Zondervan, 2023.
Identifiers: LCCN 2023013028 (print) | LCCN 2023013029 (ebook) | ISBN 9780310366478 (hardcover) | ISBN 9780310366485 (ebook)
Subjects: LCSH: Suffering—Religious aspects—Christianity. | Anxiety—Religious aspects—Christianity. | Hope—Religious aspects—Christianity. | BISAC: RELIGION / Christian Living / Death, Grief, Bereavement | RELIGION / Christian Living / Personal Growth
Classification: LCC BV4909 .T485 2023 (print) | LCC BV4909 (ebook) | DDC 248.8/6—dc23/eng/20230517
LC record available at https://lccn.loc.gov/2023013028
LC ebook record available at https://lccn.loc.gov/2023013029

Published in association with the literary agency of Nunn Communications, Inc.

Cover design: Micah Kandros
Cover photos: daniilphotos / Bernulius / Shutterstock
Interior design: Sara Colley

Printed in the United States of America

23 24 25 26 27 LBC 5 4 3 2 1

For
Leslie Nunn Reed

Whose many decades of support as my friend
and literary agent have been
immeasurably valuable

CONTENTS

Introduction: Into the Deepest Place.............. xi

1. Just Faith... 1
2. A Declaration of War—and Peace................ 18
3. A Wide Place to Stand 39
4. Glory... 55
5. Suffering: The Story of the Present Age........... 69
6. Perseverance.................................... 102
7. Character.. 132
8. Hope... 164
9. Full Circle....................................... 184

Acknowledgments............................. 205
Notes.. 208

INTO THE
DEEPEST PLACE

◆

Over the course of walking with many patients who have committed themselves to doing the difficult, often excruciating work of living, I have on many occasions witnessed transformation both glorious and durable for which words fail me. The stories within which this transformation has taken place are as varied as the people who tell them. The depth and duration of the traumas that accompany those stories are equally varied, some seemingly slight, some unspeakably gruesome.

Some stories appear in their first telling to be straightforward and uncomplicated. Only later do haunting details reveal that the patient had thus far in life been exerting some form of supernatural force to contain an emotional leviathan. Far below immediate conscious awareness, they hold it down, fearing what would be unleashed upon them if they were to release it. Other stories, given the brutality of the circumstances in which they were forged and that brought them into my office, appear at first to be ones of insurmountable odds, only to become the grist for the equally surprising development of resilience and joy.

Nevertheless, no matter the circumstances of any story at first telling, one thing that each person shares in common who has done the work that creates lasting change leading to greater love, joy, peace, patience, kindness, goodness, faithfulness, gentleness, and self-control is that he or she has suffered. This is not to suggest that only these people have suffered. For it is fair to say that to be human is to suffer. We all do.

However, what sets these people apart is that they have, to a person, developed a relationship with suffering in which they do not intentionally invite it into their lives but neither do they reject it. They have come to understand that they cannot escape suffering in life, so they no longer attempt to do so. They neither deny it nor become overwhelmed by it. Rather, they learn to be with it and acknowledge that it is with them.

But many discover that their suffering has taken up residence in the deepest places of their souls. Like many of us, they have adapted mechanisms to survive in the world of their families of origin, which they then carry on in their current relationships. To adapt, they had to bury their suffering so far below the surface that they were barely aware of its presence. Hence, to be present to and be with their suffering, they must go to the deepest places of their lives.

They do not develop this capacity—this gift, if you will—of hospitality toward their suffering without having to pass through anger, resentment, and sometimes even despair.

Indeed, to be *with* suffering, one will become well acquainted with it. This will entail becoming familiar with all of the emotional and physical manifestations that their suffering comprises—and then purposefully naming those manifestations to willing listeners who are fully present with the sufferer in the process.

Effectively naming their suffering is crucial. The ability to transform their suffering and be transformed by their experience of suffering directly correlates to the degree to which, over time, they are deeply, truly known by others in the face of it. Through these witnesses, they sense the presence of Jesus—whose body mitigates our suffering in ways that are as mysterious as they are real. As we will see, through this relational process they learn what it means to become people of hope—hope that itself circles back around to become integral to—if not the center of—that very transformational process.

Moreover, these individuals learn that hope is, perhaps surprisingly, something one *forms*. It does not plop into our laps out of the sky. It is not determined solely by our constitution or temperament. It is not optimism. And as we will see in the course of this book, it is something that only ever becomes durable through the course of suffering.

It is through the development of deeply connected relationships that they come to discover that suffering is, counterintuitively, one of the key features of our world that God uses to bring about the lasting transformation that we who follow Jesus claim that we want in our lives.

This is not the posture toward suffering that the world generally holds. Both Eastern and Western metaphysics tend to see suffering as something that needs to be either eradicated or escaped.[1] Which, on the surface of things, makes sense. Who would, under any circumstances, choose to suffer for its own sake?

In the world in which many of us believe we live—one in which either God doesn't exist, or if he does, he certainly doesn't care about the enormity of the suffering we endure—the only way to understand suffering would be as a painful, meaningless reality of what it means to be human. It must also, of course, be said that doing what we can to reduce or eliminate suffering as we are able has been, and continues to be, an undeniably noble venture. Even the hint that suffering might serve a purpose that is not merely helpful but *necessary* in the redemption of the world evokes, emotionally and culturally, virtually anaphylactic responses.

However, for people who are serious about durable transformation, they eventually develop a very different relationship with suffering from the allergic one described above. They have discovered that, in the relational economy of the God of the Bible, suffering serves, in part, a redemptive role like no other human experience. Not that this makes suffering a good thing in and of itself. Rather, this experience that we avoid and find so heinous offers the very catalyst through which the God of the Bible brings forth the new creation of beauty and goodness.

Amazingly, he transforms the very people who are wracked by suffering. In fact, he not only uses suffering as a means of redemption but, in so doing, redeems suffering itself. How is this possible to imagine, let alone realize in our bodies of bone and blood?

To do that—to imagine and engage suffering as the way of redemption—is the purpose of this book. Mind you, it does not seek to reveal new ways to respond to suffering never before considered. Indeed, nothing is new under the sun, and much has been written and lived by people far wiser and more familiar with suffering than I am.

My simple desire, rather, is to remind us of what has been understood for three millennia or more about the nature of suffering and that the way forward is through it—not around it—all within relationships. Reintroducing ourselves to the nature of relationships in the context of suffering can transform not only our relationships but our experience of suffering as well.

The primary vehicle that will carry us in our journey will be the first five verses of the fifth chapter of Paul's letter to the church at Rome. Paul writes as one who is unsurprised, even perhaps expectant, that suffering is naturally a part of the church body's life together. As I mentioned above, modern people do not live as if suffering is the norm, to be expected. We think it an anomaly in the universe, a wrinkle in the matrix. Paul and the people of the early Jesus movement knew better. For they knew the world as it really was. As it really is. A world in which suffering is to be anticipated—and to which followers of Jesus are to respond accordingly.

It is my intention that as this book unfolds, you will be drawn in by the progression of Paul's words and will come to discover what my patients who are doing the hard work of living have also discovered: through suffering we form hope. Durable hope. Not the hope that for me is often flimsier than I would like to admit. For indeed, given my life of affluence that affords me a virtually limitless selection of options to distract myself from my pain, I have not often been required to practice putting in the actual effort required to form hope. Consequently, hope that feels as fragile as mine often isn't really much to put my hope in.

But I assume I am not alone in not having formed durable hope as well as I would have liked. In fact, the culture in which we live has trained us to become increasingly fragile. Research on the development of resilience suggests that successive generations over the last forty years have found themselves less and less able to be hopeful about the future because they lack the interior emotional and relational architecture necessary to do so.[2]

Sturdy relational architecture grows and is strengthened by first encountering minimal forms of suffering, then gradually tolerating it to greater and greater degrees. In this process of facing and doing hard things, durable hope is realized. We cannot form hope that is able to weather the storms of our lives if we are unwilling to encounter the suffering that today's culture attempts to deliver us from at all costs.

But that isn't all. Just because I read in the Bible that suffering can somehow lead to hope does not make me any more optimistic that it's possible, let alone likely. Such belief is drowned by the other voices that constantly tell me that I should be able to have life how, when, and where I want it. I should not have to suffer, and if I do, the message is clear: there is something wrong with the world that is not doing for me what I deserve.

Fortunately, along with the biblical text, we will also examine the other ways God speaks to us to reveal who he is and how he works in the world, not least when it comes to suffering and hope. Paul informs his readers early in his letter to the church at Rome that the creation itself tells us of God's power and his nature, and that people have been aware of this from the beginning.[3] Part of that good creation includes the way that God has intended our brains, minds, and relationships to work in concert with each other so that we love one another well and create and curate beauty and goodness in the world.

Interpersonal neurobiology (IPNB) is the field of study that draws together findings of various scientific disciplines that have a stake in understanding the nature of a flourishing mind. As a psychiatrist working with patients at the intersection of IPNB and Christian spiritual formation, I have seen how the application of the findings of neuroscience have enriched the comprehension and experience of the biblical texts and enabled us to even more effectively live out the life of wisdom that the Bible calls us to.

It is my intention to weave together the biblical narrative, interpersonal neurobiology, and the stories of the people you will meet—all of which converge in the context of healing relational communities to which I will introduce you. Not only will the resulting tapestry lead us to discover what it means to tolerate suffering, but through the formation of hope we will learn what it means to be transformed by it while bearing witness to how our suffering itself is redeemed.

If you are skeptical or downright incredulous that there is anything hopeful to even be considered, let alone discovered and tactically applied in the presence of our suffering, I want to say that your doubt only makes sense. When we look around at our world, how could one possibly think otherwise and still be considered sane? Each one of us, merely looking at our own life that seems to take so long to change (not to mention the violence we see all around us), finds the need to cry out, "How long, LORD? Will you forget me forever? How long will you hide your face from me?"[4]

Here, I can only bear witness to the work of the Spirit in creating beauty and goodness in the deepest places of suffering and in ways I would not have imagined possible. The lives of people you will meet here evidence these possibilities happening in real time and space. They can happen for you, too, because our hope is ultimately not an abstraction nor is it in our own personal agency to transform ourselves. Rather, hope lies in Another. It is in Jesus, the hope of glory.[5]

And with *that* hope in mind, let's begin.

Chapter One

JUST FAITH

◆

Therefore, since we have been justified through faith,
we have peace with God through our Lord Jesus Christ,
through whom we have gained access by faith into this
grace in which we now stand. And we boast in the hope
of the glory of God. Not only so, but we also glory in our
sufferings, because we know that suffering produces
perseverance; perseverance, character; and character,
hope. And hope does not put us to shame, because God's
love has been poured out into our hearts through the
Holy Spirit, who has been given to us.

ROMANS 5:1–5

Max's interminable ruminations, always worrying about
never getting it right, never being good enough in his
career, had the effect of both sweeping him into the fast track
of advancement—because of how hard he worked in response

1

to his worry—and leading him to accumulate a life of misery along the way.

Carmina was married to a man who, committed as he was to the tenets of their faith, had no commitment whatsoever to being curious about his inner life or his outer harshness that he frequently directed at her in public, leaving her to a life of longing and languishing, trapped in a dry well of sadness and despair.

Edwin's autoimmune arthritic condition had, over twenty years, slowly done everything but kill him. He didn't want to die. But he had a hard time wanting to live.

Karen lost her husband in Afghanistan and her son to a drug overdose. Now she most feared losing her very soul to the subsequent continual pain of loss that she perceived as nearly too much to bear.

Westin's serial infidelities had corrupted everyone and everything around him. The very thought of an intimate relationship, despite his desperate longing for one, only compounded his shame and his fear of that very thing he most longed for. Shame and fear that consumed most of his waking hours.

Paulina had done hard, effective spiritual and emotional work for several years, developing resilience and joy on so many fronts. Why, then, did the old, familiar family story continue to haunt her, blindsiding her at the most inopportune times, leaving her emotionally distraught for days on end?

Time in prison was one thing. Living with the shame of it after being released was worse. What was Garrett to do with the incessant battering his mind had to withstand simply to get from the morning to the night as he tried to forget his past?

◆ ◆ ◆

To be human is to suffer. Indeed, suffering was at the center of the experiences of each of the people whose stories you just read. It was ultimately, in fact, what prompted and escorted them into my office. Moreover, hope felt desperately out of reach, often perceived as a mirage that evaporated anytime any of them was engulfed with the images and sensations of their affliction. But although it was perceived to be beyond them, hope was not completely out of their visual field, or they would not have been speaking with me in the first place. However, it only flitted through their peripheral vision; suffering—and the attendant story that they were telling about it—most often occupied their direct sight line.

Certainly, each person's suffering is unique to the individual; with a nod to Tolstoy, each of us is unhappy—we suffer—in our own particular way.[1] At the same time, the suffering of those chronicled above shared common characteristics we will explore in detail later in this book. However, beyond our awareness that all suffering shares common attributes, most important is the reality that we *all* suffer, even if we are often quite extraordinarily unaware of it.

As we will eventually see, the question is not *if* we each suffer. It is, rather, *To what degree are we aware of it?* and *How are we in relationship with and responding to it?* These questions reveal not only the story we believe we are living in, but the role that suffering plays in that narrative.

You have chosen to read this book for any number of reasons. You may be one who suffers, and you know it. Or perhaps you know someone else who suffers, and you want to help

3

them. Or you may be curious about suffering but don't think you encounter it that often or that deeply and have questions about why that is. Perhaps you wonder if the pain you hold qualifies as suffering and want to know if you are permitted to name it as such. In the face of your suffering or that of others, you long to discover and maintain hope, all the while attempting to make sense of the suffering in the process.

But I will tell you why I would likely want to read a book, any book, about suffering. At some level, I am hoping that I will discover how I will be able to suffer less. Less painfully. Less often. I want to know more about suffering so that I can have less of it in my life. Of course, it's okay if I learn some things about it along the way—but again, only if what I learn helps me mitigate it.

If I am going to read a book about suffering and hope, I would anticipate that the first step would be either to understand suffering or, even better, to discover solutions for it, so that at the end of the day in some way I actually won't have to suffer as much as I might otherwise. And therein would lie the hope. Why would I want to read something that would merely validate and reinforce the message, "Yes, you're right. Suffering is hard. End of story." Where is there any hope in that message?

I want to be hopeful. Hopeful that I have agency to diminish my suffering. Because, I admit, I don't easily comprehend how hope and suffering coexist in my mind and life. But one of the things we will learn over the course of this book is that, from the standpoint of the biblical narrative and in light of what we are discovering about neuroscience, suffering— while not God's ideal intention—is a *necessary* element in our becoming our truest, most beautiful, most heaven-ready selves. It is an unavoidable reality of life. One that God plainly does not fully deliver us from in the time frame we would like, if ever.

Moreover, it is a reality that he seems just as plainly committed to using suffering—for reasons that are a great mystery to me—to transform us into who he wants us to become. However, it remains something that I most often choose to avoid if possible instead of accepting it as having anything to do with becoming who I actually long to be.

All of this is both very hard and very good news. It's easy to imagine why it is hard. But to approach understanding how in any universe it could be good will require what may be a severe overhaul of our imaginations. This book intends to address what is required for us to form deeply embedded, durable hope, not only in the presence of our pain but as a direct result of it.

I make no promise that we will suffer less. But I am confident that we will suffer *differently* and will become even more durably hopeful as a result. Primarily, I expect us to come to see that hope is actually a word that, in the world of inter-personal neurobiology, serves as a proxy for an ever-deepening attachment love with Jesus and the commensurate awareness of God's relational presence of lovingkindness. But more on that later.

To arrive at that place of being securely attached to Jesus in this way, however, our journey, necessarily and somewhat counterintuitively, begins not with suffering itself but rather with what precedes it. For it is often most helpful, when wanting to understand a "problem," to begin at the beginning. And perhaps at a place that may surprise us.

BEGINNING AT THE BEGINNING

We are people who encounter the world first through our senses. We eventually develop the capacity to *think about* our world, but we first *encounter* our world as sensing beings. Hans Urs von Balthasar sheds significant theological and philosophical light on this. His work provides important, necessary grounding for apprehending what neuroscience reveals to us about the general pattern of brain function.[2] Von Balthasar reminds us that it is beauty that draws our senses to our awareness of the world, and only later do we think about it. This is true for our suffering as well; first we sense it, and only then do we think about it. In the language of IPNB, this means "later" both in terms of our neurological development as well as in how our brains work in real time. First we sense things, such as my finger on the hot stove burner; and then I become aware in my "thoughts" that I am experiencing pain. Later on I will introduce you to the notion of how suffering has to do with our perception of time, particularly how we perceive and anticipate our future.

We expect our future to reflect what we most long for—and those deep longings commence at birth. Hence, one way to consider suffering is as the severe, painful frustration of our desires. I don't typically imagine that being able to stand up from my chair in a single, smooth motion would be one of my deepest desires. But when my lower back seizes and I am unable to stand without great pain and only with careful movement, I am thrust into a situation in which I desire nothing more desperately than to be able to move without pain. Here we see how suffering emerges as a function of thwarted desire, even ones we have little awareness of having. But long before those desires are frustrated, they are formed in the earliest stages of development.

From the time we are born, we initially *sense* the world—both inside and outside our skin—and only then do we begin to perceive and give meaning to what we are sensing. In this way, first we sense, and then we make sense of what we sense.[3] This follows the axiom that the brain, in general, operates from bottom to top and then right to left, meaning that we generally receive input sensations through our spinal cord or our cranial nerves, all of which first lead to the lower parts of our brains.

When it comes to neural impulses coming from our limbs, what we sense on one side of the body (a pinprick, pain, or cold) sends signals to the opposite side of the brain. Signals from my right side travel eventually to my left brain and vice versa. When it comes to what I sense *inside* my body, the nervous system operates somewhat differently. After ascending to the lower brain, these impulses mostly travel to the right hemisphere and from there travel across the corpus callosum to the left hemisphere, where the combined work of the right and left prefrontal cortices enable us to "make sense" of what we initially "sense."[4]

Granted, even this oversimplified description is important to keep in mind as we approach the topic of suffering and move closer and closer to hope. When it comes to suffering, before we "make sense" of it, we first must address what, exactly, we are sensing.

This process of the mind, considering the brain's bottom-to-top and right-to-left neural connectivity, eventually culminates in the development of the middle prefrontal cortex, the physical locale that is most highly correlated with what emerge as uniquely human abilities. But for this dimension of our physical development to emerge into what we describe in the terms of interpersonal biology as an integrated life, a flourishing life, it requires the context of a secure attachment between the child and his or her parent.[5]

Developing secure attachment is itself the interpersonal neurobiological process by which we are primed to be receptive to what Moses and Jesus described—to love God with all of our heart, mind, soul, and strength—as well as what is described in Paul's letter to the Galatians as a life bearing the fruit of the Spirit.[6] Moreover, secure attachment is the relational vehicle by which hope begins to form in us as children and continues to develop throughout our lives.

Attachment is the embodied and relational dance between child and parent in which "hope" as an abstract, cognitively imagined "thing" eventually emerges as something the child can *think about*. This is possible only after the child has experienced enough emotional outcomes enabling them to feel seen, soothed, safe, and secure (collectively known as the 4 S's),[7] not least in the presence of difficult situations. Through these experiences, he or she begins to anticipate a future of comfort and confidence. In other words, the child first must develop a predictable, durable *sense* of things that enables her to anticipate a future of goodness before she *thinks about* her future as one that is hopeful.

Keeping all of this in mind, we now turn to the initial phrase of Romans chapter 5, "Therefore, since we have been justified through faith . . ." In this case, to be justified—to be the recipient of God's justification—is essentially, as N. T. Wright indicates, to hear from God that we are "in the right" or in good standing with him.[8]

In essence, we hear him say, "I love you and want to be with you and have you be with me in our family. Jesus's faithful actions are the embodied demonstration of that. *And* it is up to you to trust me that this is true by living as if it's true." God declares that in and through the faithful work of Jesus as Messiah, we are being welcomed into his family, invited to have a seat at his table—*and* our faith, our *trust*, in God's promise that this is true is the necessary mechanism, or conduit, by which we actively receive it.[9] God has offered what we could never imagine, let alone offer ourselves—*and* we must be receptive to it. And therein lies the rub.

Some of us have heard or read this text in Paul's letter to the Romans so often that it may not penetrate any further than our mind's assent to having read some words on a page. For when it comes to "faith," we often imagine it primarily as a theological concept, one having to do with the world of cognitive assent. I "believe" tends to mean that I affirm, in the way I rationally think, that something is "true." Such as that one plus one equals two, that Columbus is the capital of Ohio, or that the world is round (or so I have been told). But this would be taking in Paul's meaning with only a part of our mind and not with the most significant functional element.

As with any relationship, our relationship with God begins and is maintained via the process of attachment described above. Spiritual director Anne Halley puts a finer point on the dance between parents and their children and then, eventually, between adults in all sorts of relationally intimate settings, when she describes secure attachment as the process by which the newborn, infant, and child becomes increasingly aware of and attuned to the awareness and attunement of their parent directed toward them with lovingkindness.[10] This highlights how attachment is, necessarily and primarily, an *embodied* encounter.

For example, consider the social engagement system (SES). The SES is a complex constellation of neural networks that each of us is born with but that is immature at birth. This system activates multiple physical and emotional responses (e.g., facial expression, emotional tone, body language, tone of voice, physical touch, and perception of the parent's intention, to name a few) and enables a child and parent to interact in such a way that the child grows in his capacity to tolerate distressing emotional states.

The SES grows in maturity over time through ongoing interactions with the parent in which the parent is attuned to the mind of the child in ways that grow the child's emotional resilience. We each have a particular capacity to tolerate distressing affect. This capacity is described as one's window of tolerance (WOT). Growth in emotional and relational maturity is therefore measured in terms of the widening of one's WOT, another way of describing the growth of one's emotional resilience.[11]

The SES is one example, via our embodied and relational minds, of *how* we actually develop the capacity to "trust" in the first place. Before we can "trust" or "have faith in" God, we first must practice and strengthen our mind's capacity to trust at all. Again, "trust" or "faith" is a word that represents most primally an interpersonal, embodied interaction in which we are being ever more deeply known and thereby loved.

We often limit what we call "faith" or "faith in God" to a rational, cognitive assent to a set of abstract principles, ones that could be found in the Apostles' Creed, for example. I say I trust God when in fact what I mean is that I trust in a rational collection of cognitive beliefs. This is much like believing the fact that airplanes can fly because I have read about it or seen them do so. But God desires for us to board the plane in order for us to become airborne.

This in no way diminishes the role of the creeds nor our use of rational cognition when it comes to our relationships. It merely places them in their proper sequence. There are many times, in fact, when I must use logical, linear cognitive processing to guide my sensing, embodied states of mind in the direction I want them to go. But our relationships do not begin as, nor are they maintained *primarily* as, a function of the mind's capacity for abstract thinking.

The early construction of hope and our eventual capacity to endure suffering must first be grounded in materially real relationships—ones that begin with our primary attachment figures and then extend to God as we encounter him—relationships that we sense in our embodied experience and that are not limited merely to a set of cognitive principles.

At this point I'd like to invite you to pause and direct your attention to what you perceive your embodied responses to be when you consider what it means to "trust" God. Your embodied responses are what you sense in your body upon imagining Jesus telling you, "Indeed, it is finished. It's all done. All those things that we both know keep you from receiving my love for you—I'm not paying attention to them. I'm paying attention to you. And I want you to only pay attention to me. I want you at my banquet. I want you sitting right next to me and to the others who I know can't wait to sit next to you when they see you. I would love for you to believe me—that it's all true."

How difficult is it to receive that? What do you sense, imagine, feel, think, and want to do physically in response to hearing Jesus say this? Moreover, were you to imagine such an encounter, could you receive it as having represented something genuine, something real that has taken place in the real world? Or, since we have come to believe that if we are imagining something "in our minds" then it could not possibly "exist" as a real event in the real world, would you dismiss it?

We have been trained by many cultural forces over the last five hundred years to believe that if something can't be currently measured in material terms, if it is limited to the "imagination," then it can't be "real." But you know that just because you can't see your friend sitting before you and can only imagine their face and the sound of their voice in your mind, they are not merely imaginary.

What are we to do with findings of research that demonstrate how athletes and musicians can enhance their performance on the court or in the concert hall by repeatedly practicing those very actions *in their imaginations*?[12] They are effectively shifting their embodied responses in certain contexts (the athletic court and the concert hall) by wiring their brains to anticipate those very scenarios. In this way, their brains—from which emerge the functional feature of their imaginations and their conscious awareness of them—and then, by extension, the actions they take as a result are essentially on a continuum, connected as they are within their bodies and to the intentionality of the musician or athlete.

Similarly, who of your friends could tell you how they feel about you and you would live, at least for the next few hours, as if you believed them? As if what you felt in your chest was *real.* On more occasions than I can tell you, people have told me how much I mean to them, how much they love me, only for their words and presence to vanish like vapor from my mind the moment they are no longer in my sight.

I am left with only the memory of what they have said and what I sensed, imaged (that is, to literally construct a visual image in my mind), felt, and thought as they said it—and often the memory is not durable enough for me to sustain the same felt sense of their affection for me which I had for that brief moment. Hence, I have to *practice*—literally—bringing those moments to memory over and over in order for them to become embedded not only in my cognitive recollection but in my embodied sensations, feelings, and images as well.

In this way, by practicing with real, embodied relationships in my here-and-now life, I am granted what it gets close to being like when I imagine Jesus coming for me in the same way. This is how the body of Jesus works, and it is why Paul's words of us being Jesus's *body*, and not merely his followers or his church, capture everything that we are to become for each other and the world. And it is why hope is first given life in the context of securely attached, physically remembered relationships rather than being merely a function of our cognition.

Michael, one of my patients, had what he considered to be a long-standing relationship with God, which was not untrue. It was equally true that God was *something* that he mostly thought *about*. God was less *someone with whom* Michael had a relationship. His perceived, sensed awareness of God's *presence* remained further out of his reach than he wanted, than he so deeply hungered and thirsted for.

He was able to speak genuinely of his longing to love and be loved by God. Moreover, he was acutely aware of how deeply his current life circumstances and the emotionally overwhelming nature of them made it virtually impossible for him to access a sense of God's love, despite his deeply held, cognitive conviction of its reality. His suffering was plainly evident, as his medical condition and the stresses of his unforgiving work setting occupied the forefront of his mind.

He was able to accept in theory the notion that secure attachment—to be seen, soothed, safe, and secure (the 4 S's)—is important. But how was he to realize what seemed outside of his capacity to imagine, let alone put into practice?

Michael desperately longed for hope—what emerges, as we will see, as our anticipated future as a function of secure attachment. And I was confident that he would eventually realize it and do so in even more durable ways than he had been before entering into psychotherapy with me.

One way to approach this possibility is through the work accomplished within a confessional community. These are ongoing groups of patients (or in some cases, groups that voluntarily form apart from our practice and are not supervised by therapists, but that have received training in how to begin and maintain them), usually six to eight in number, that are facilitated by two of our therapists whose purpose is to enable group members to tell their stories more truly. They ultimately do the work of spiritual formation using the tools of group psychotherapy dynamics and principles of IPNB, all of which are informed by an understanding of life as shaped by the biblical narrative.[13]

When Michael became a member of one of these groups at our practice, the therapists and other group members were curious about how and where in his body he sensed things as he navigated moments of emotional vulnerability. During the course of his work in the community, he first began to practice reimagining encounters of empathy and even difficult confrontations. He eventually grew to tolerate and even welcome these interactions with the other members, all of which were largely navigated with care and kindness.

There came a point at which we invited him to imagine Jesus joining the rest of the community in his imagination—taking, as it were, the community with him, Jesus included, into those moments in which he needed to know he was not alone. It was a revelation to him that, prior to this, he had rarely attuned to these very sensations, images, and feelings when he encountered God in prayer (or if he did, he never understood them to be "real").

But when he began to practice imagining his entire mind's experience being revealed to Jesus—as he was regularly doing in the confessional community—he was able to have an embodied encounter with Jesus as well. All of the compassion and serious care that Jesus offered to Michael in those moments effectively regulated Michael's distress cycle—what he sensed, imaged, or felt.

In this way, Michael had an *embodied encounter* with the *body* of Christ as Paul describes it in 1 Corinthians 12. We have become disconnected enough from the material world that we often limit, albeit unconsciously, to sheer metaphor what Paul refers to and assumes to be the body of Christ. (I use the word "nonconscious" to denote those activities of the mind that we are not aware of, which could be any number of things. And I use it rather than the more commonly used "unconscious," the technical term coined by Sigmund Freud that referred to a particular psychoanalytic domain of the mind. My use of the word "nonconscious" is more inclusive than what Freud was referring to.)

Yes, the body metaphor truly reflects who we are and what we are to be, but the notion of us being literally, materially one *body* is not easy for us to fully appreciate or appropriate. This is merely one way in which we do not attune to the serious-ness with which the Trinity takes us as his church and intends for us—*in our very bodies*—to convey the presence of Jesus to each other and to the world. Apart from our assent to it as a theological abstraction, we have limited attunement to God's attunement to us.

Michael came to trust—to *have faith*—in Jesus by trusting his embodied sensations and perceptions that he practiced in the community—Jesus's very body. He made the connec-tion between his experience in the community and the way it primed him to have the encounter with Jesus that he did. In this way, he came to make sense of what it means *in the mate-rial world* to be "justified by faith."

He did not simply cognitively assent to this as a posited theological notion. Rather, in this very concrete, embodied fash-ion, Michael's *faith* (sensed, imaged, felt, thought, and behaved/embodied trust) in God's *declaration that in Jesus's death and resurrection all has been made right and Michael is wanted and welcome in God's family* (justification) was becoming ever more grounded in the material world. This was his embodied process of attachment. His encounter with and receptivity to the community opened the door for him to trust with all of his mind—his entire embodied and relational self—that God had

"justified" him and made "justification" a lived—and living—
phenomenon for Michael.

Hope—the future state of time that our minds long to
occupy—must begin with a relationally grounded, material experience with Jesus mediated through the Spirit, the
Scriptures, and, often most powerfully, his body. We become
increasingly receptive, experientially and thereby theologically, to our having been justified—declared free of our guilt
and shame and welcomed into God's family—to the degree that
we encounter that justification in an embodied fashion, one in
which we are ever living into earned secure attachment.[14] Upon
this taking place, the prospect of hope—even in the presence of
suffering—begins to form in our minds.

But evil never rests. And the next chapter reminds us not
only that this is so but also that so much of our attention is frequently and unconsciously drawn, not to God's declaration of
joy over us, but to something very much its opposite.

Chapter Two

A DECLARATION OF WAR—AND PEACE

◆

... we have peace with God through
our Lord Jesus Christ ...

ROMANS 5:1B

From the beginning, life in this world has been the way of
violence. Perhaps not the *very* beginning. But it didn't take
long. Before any fruit was eaten from the tree of the knowledge
of good and evil, the serpent violated the woman's relationship
with God, wounding it with shame.[1] Shame that was subtle but
violent—*violating*—nonetheless. Although the text of Genesis
reads plainly that it was Eve whom the serpent wounded
directly through its deception, the text also alludes that this
wounding took place in the presence of Adam, that he "was
with her,"[2] he to whom the original directive forbidding them

to eat of the fruit of the tree of the knowledge of good and evil was given.

It is significant that the writers of Genesis imply in the text that the only way Eve would have known that the fruit was forbidden was for Adam to tell her. Given her response to the serpent's initial inquiry, it appears that communication between her and her husband is already somewhat imperfect, not unlike a game of whisper down the lane.[3] Not unlike the experience of many of us in our families.

The couple demonstrates how vulnerable to their humanity they are, like any of us, in having to learn how to convey information clearly and comprehensively, especially very important information. This is not about sin. This is about being nascently human.

Through this nascence, evil takes advantage in committing violence toward the first couple. Eve's trauma was by direct assault; Adam's was by witnessing it happening to her— what we would call secondary or vicarious trauma[4]—yet doing nothing about it.

We see in the text that the serpent did not begin the conversation with both the man and the woman, let alone wait to have it when God came along for his walk in the garden. Rather, he directed his words to only one of them, the one who was one step removed from God's direct command about the forbidden tree, the one more dependent on another human to know what God had said.

The snake thereby isolates Eve in the conversation, albeit in the presence of her husband. How many times have any of us felt the same way—isolated while standing in a sea of people, even those with whom we long to be close? By directing the dialogue in this way, the serpent is already separating them from each other and from God. And it is this isolation that is the first step that leads to war.

The text implies that in response to the serpent's argument Eve chose between God and *her* coping mechanism—the fruit. Adam chose between God and *his* coping mechanism—his wife. As Eve made a choice between who—God or her—would be the final authority about what is right and wrong, she did not make it in a vacuum. She appears unaware of God's utter delight in her. She acts instead in response to a wound of shame that the serpent inflicted.[5]

This subtle attack was effective. The context of her choice was not a pain-free environment. Moreover, we see from Adam's silence that she did not receive any assistance from him. In her perception, she was left alone to cope with her distress by choosing either God's way or the fruit, which would provide nourishment, pleasure, wisdom, and power,[6] power perhaps to which she perceived she otherwise did not have access.

On the other hand, Adam observed this conversation, yet remained aloof. We are not told why, only that he was with her. He remained static in his posture toward the whole affair with no apparent attempt to intercede on her behalf or tell the serpent to get lost. And when, after she had taken and eaten and then offered him some as well, he too faced a choice.

Adam knew that death was at his doorstep—or so he had been told. But he was not now faced with merely choosing directly between God and the fruit. He was not having to "take" fruit from the tree. He was being "given" it. And being given it by the one who had been given to him so that he would not be alone.

To refuse the fruit from Eve was therefore not just saying no to the fruit; it was saying no to his wife. To the very creation that had evoked the beauty of song and poetry only one page earlier in the Bible.

Yes, he was choosing his own way rather than God's. But what he would lose by allowing God to be in charge of what is right and wrong—his wife of comfort, of beauty, of joy—was a bridge too far. And so, by choosing the fruit, he chose his wife—or so he thought. In reality, he had been primarily acting to reduce his own distress. Had he truly been choosing his wife, he would have done so much earlier in the conversation. For reasons the writers do not provide, something about the way the serpent was isolating Eve also affected Adam. This is the way of the violence of shame. And this is the path to war.

Shortly after their indulgence, indeed, their eyes "were opened."[7] Yet not only *what* but *how* they saw was not what they expected. This was not what they thought the serpent meant when he told them their vision would be like God's.[8] Their nakedness was off-putting. More specifically, they were off-putting to each other. The war had begun without the couple yet being fully aware of where this was leading—not unlike a single assassination that led to what became World War I.

Their newfound eyesight immediately moves them even further away from each other. They respond by covering their nakedness. Their sin next affects their hearing, as even that—*hearing* God walking in the cool of the day—elicits anxiety where once it would have evoked anticipated joy. In response, they scurry into the woods, where they are not only hidden from God but even further hidden from one another.

When God shows up on the scene, Adam throws Eve

under the bus, and what follows—with God's declaration of how their behavior will have a perpetual downstream cursed effect on everything—is to be expected, yet only in hindsight. What began with the violence the serpent directed explicitly upon the woman and implicitly upon the man was followed by violence perpetrated between the woman and the man in their words and actions and extended a mere chapter later in Genesis in the murder of one brother by another. And so it has ever been.

I don't offer these reflections cavalierly or naively. Neither am I presenting an exegesis of this text—a theological or anthropological explanation of the human origin of sin. Rather, I draw your attention to all that is anciently woven into the fabric of human suffering.

But the God of the Bible stands at the ready to redeem any and all things. We will eventually see hope imagined and realized in the face of *and as a function of that very suffering.* Suffering that is ancient not only for us as a race but that many of you may feel is as ancient as your life's duration. Suffering that has come as a result of the violation of something in your life and over which you have no control, no capacity to regulate. Yet this suffering will also become the catalyst for the formation of hope and the center of God's transforming power.

Since the first violation involved God (he made the serpent, after all; and the serpent blamed God in his wounding of the woman), we have set him up as the source of pain. Like Adam, we blame him as the most responsible party for all the ills of our world, and it is with him that we wage war more deeply and historically than anyone else. We ultimately believe that God is at war with us, and like Adam and Eve we believe he is coming to kill us. No wonder, then, that when we had the chance, we killed him when we killed Jesus.

To repeat, this compelling story of our first parents sweeps us up so much in the drama of the characters that we often forget not only how God was involved in the abstract but that all of these events took place well within the earshot of God, who conveniently shows up for his evening walk just past the nick of time.

You, the reader, are well acquainted with the conversation that ensues. Adam infamously accuses God, effectively blaming him for the entire debacle. Adam directs his anger (which is coming to the defense of his shame) toward the one he finds ultimately responsible for his actions. What follows?

God names what will become of humanity and the ground upon which they walk because they chose to decide for themselves what is right and wrong, no matter the consequences to others. They instigate curses applied universally to people, to nonhuman living things, and to the earth.

This led to further violence when Cain murdered Abel. This action in no small part represents an extended generational trauma, one in which the children were acting out the unfinished business of the violence between their parents. And so we see how violence begets violence.

In these first events of humanity, we recognize that our easier, natural tendency is a path of violence. It requires far more energy, far more effort to turn away wrath with a soft response than it does to respond in like manner. Violence is easy. Peacemaking is herculean.

This was true for a couple I counseled, Celeste and Wes. They lived in a marriage to which they were committed, but

Celeste's history of unresolved trauma led to a vicious cycle in their interactions. Her implicit memory of feeling continually criticized and ignored fed her responses whenever Wes "simply" responded to her expressions of emotion with his "suggestions" for how she could feel better by simply understanding the situation in a more rational manner.

His take on the situations only further ignited Celeste's rage, which led to Wes's withdrawal, which strengthened her rage . . . a cycle that devolved into emotional carnage with the two of them not speaking with each other for several days.

John Gottman's research on marriage[9] and the work that Sue Johnson and colleagues have established with the development of emotionally focused therapy[10] help us understand that Wes and Celeste felt powerless to change the course of their arguments midstream. Over time, they had become unable to regulate the emotional elements of their relationship that were driving so much of how they related.

We will explore in more detail later what it means to widen the "window of emotional tolerance" as we regulate our autonomic nervous system. For now, it is enough to know that our brains work in such a way that we are committed to guaranteeing safety in the world before we do much of anything else.

For indeed, how does one plant crops or write novels or teach or compose music if you fundamentally perceive yourself to be in danger? The brain stem and amygdala—the primitive parts of our brains that we have in common phylogenetically with reptiles and lower mammals—constantly work to monitor the landscape, both externally and internally, looking for danger. We scan for not merely physical danger but also what our memory records as emotionally threatening experiences. These parts of our brain command our fight-or-flight system.

Unless we are committed to regulating those parts of our brain with the help of our prefrontal cortex—the part of our brain that most sets us apart as humans—our reaction to threat will be to flee or to fight. What this means in practice is that when we can't flee, violence is a far easier option than peacemaking.

In all of our wars with each other, we have been at war with God from the beginning as well. In some ways, we direct our violence toward the "objects" that are closest to us—our spouses, children, and parents. Invariably, however, we extend it to our coworkers; those of different ethnicities, political persuasions, or social sensibilities; our enemies and our friends; even our neighboring countries. These stand in proxy for God, the One with whom we are *really* at war in the depth of our souls.

Every act of envious, lying, stealing, adulterous murder that I commit toward someone else merely holds the object of my violence as a proxy for God. Truly, in every act of treasonous sin I commit, I am, like Adam, saying to God, "The woman you gave me . . ."

Moreover, it's far easier to be in conflict with the person that is embodied and standing right in front of me because, first, it's right there in front of me; and second, it is ultimately less frightening than God, despite how little I think about how much I am at war with him. Who wants to be at war with the "ultimate" Object that has the capacity to cause me the greatest degree of suffering?

And so, if you ask me, I will tell you that I'm at war with a real human with whom I have not repaired a rupture. But if you ask me if I'm at war with God, I likely will tell you that I have no idea what you're talking about. I'm a Christian, and Christians know that God loves us. He's not at war with us.

Our sense of being at war with the gods is nothing new. Rather, it is something we inherited from our ancestors. The early religious cults of the ancient Near East portrayed the gods in terms of violence. (For that matter, so did the ancient civilizations of the Americas.)[11] The Babylonians and Persians, Greeks and Romans understood the terms of engagement with the gods who were as capricious as they were violent. And so, to fend them off or to appease them in order to ensure that they had enough food to eat or sex to enjoy or goods to trade, they offered sacrifices.

You might say that we all know that those gods didn't and don't really exist, so how could anyone be truly at war with them? As it turns out, I am quite able to be so. Moreover, perhaps the ancients were just more honest about their relationships with the gods than I am.

I, too, believe that I am at war with the gods. Or, if Richard Schwartz is correct, whose work we will touch on in just a moment, at least parts of me believe this. I map the gods of my own making—such as sex, power, the assurance of my place in society because of my profession, the comfort and convenience of my affluence, and other projections of my own heart—onto the God of gods, making him out to be a tyrant who, at the end of the day, isn't *really* interested in my welfare.

Even the very principalities and powers themselves of which Paul speaks in his letter to the Ephesians[12]—to these gods, too, I make sacrifices of time, energy, attention. I have committed so much of my energy to them, terrified as I am that they won't provide for me the money, sex, and power that I believe I need in order to be okay. And so I appease them so they will be happy to help me; for indeed, I can't afford to be at war with the gods whom I believe to be ultimately responsible for my welfare. And we have been at this war for as long as we have been humans.

Mind you, we are not always aware that we are *at war*—we think that we worship the gods because of the good they do for us. But we pay less attention to the fact that we are also terrified that the gods will *not* do for us what we want; they will *fail* us. We will then explicitly enter into the war that we have been implicitly waging for as long as we have been on the planet.

Not only this, but in our deepest place of suffering, at the center of our breath-bodies, we wonder to ourselves if that very suffering is a direct result of the war that *God* is waging with *us*. A war that we have no way of winning. The sexless marriage that remains listless and static. The parents who continue to expect you, the adult child, to be the mature person in the room and clean up the family mess that they are responsible for. The addiction to pornography you cannot overcome. The boss who looks past your hard work but easily finds ways to blame you for things that are his responsibility. The married pastor who has made sexual advances toward you, a woman married to someone else, but who, when he is confronted, dismisses your account of the facts outright.

It is not difficult in these, the deepest places of suffering, to believe, albeit quite unconsciously, that the God of the Bible is indeed at war with us. This makes hope even more difficult to imagine. Moreover, these states of conflict are rife with multiple layers of our insecure attachments affecting the larger whole of the system of our family, school, work, or church.

How many times have we experienced conflicts that began in the inner recesses of one or two persons' minds in the office or elder board or faculty that eventually spilled out into the hallways with people taking sides and taking names? That this so often happens even in our places of worship shows how much at war with each other we are, with God standing in the middle.

But the gospel tells a different story. A story of a different God than the gods we have imagined. A God who has initiated the peacemaking process. A God who has never been at war with us in the first place.

This God has been willing for us to blame him for everything that is wrong with our lives and with our world, while in fact we are responsible. He has been willing to take it, waiting for Jesus to arrive so that he could show us in real time and space, in embodied form, just how true this is.

In Jesus, God has sent the ultimate emissary of peace. Peace that must be *made*. And made, mind you, as an effort of very hard work. The story of Scripture tells us that Jesus has not just come to *make* peace—rather, he himself *is* that very peace.

Jesus is the location where and the means by which all of our wars with God and each other come to an end. He does not do this by negotiating terms—he does not negotiate. He does so by being with us in the room, telling us, in all of our warring armor, to come to him if we are weary and weighed down with the burden of our suffering selves. He invites us to take off our armor and replace it with a yoke, one that is easy.[13]

The essence of this peacemaking process is grounded in what we explored in the first chapter. God has initiated relationship with us, as he has from the beginning, and in Jesus he has now made a way for us to have an embodied connection to him through the Spirit and via his people. This healing of our hostilities in fact develops what we term in the language of IPNB earned secure attachments.

We form trust bonds in a relationship that gradually enables us to form hope, the mental state in which we anticipate a future of goodness and beauty rather than one that is a continual, pitched battle. Furthermore, we form this hope largely out of what we experience *in the present moment of being loved in embodied fashion*, not just in the abstract.[14]

It is Jesus to whom we become securely attached, and we do this via the work of the Holy Spirit and in the presence and embodied actions of Jesus's followers. His body. We do not make peace only with words and the signing of accords. And we certainly don't do it on our own. We do so with our bodies and with each other: with our tone of voice, our eye contact, our tears and smiles and laughter. Our hard working through ruptures to the place of repair. Our sharing of the Eucharist with those toward whom we felt resentful just yesterday. And God—the God of the Scriptures, not any of the other gods—is behind it all.

A significant, necessary element of developing earned secure attachment with Jesus and others includes naming our wounds. Naming where we have been and still are at war with God, with each other, and with ourselves. To name things is to tell our stories ever more truly. It is to name our longings and our griefs. It is to be explicit in describing the nature of the lives we have lived.

Moreover, our naming, our telling the stories of our lives more truly, can only be offered to other people. Yes, to Jesus, but in his relational economy, which we understand to be his body, it means we name our wounds in the presence of other fellow pilgrims. And we must do so because evil is counting on our forgetting about them.

It can be easy for us to forget that we don't live in a neutral universe. We can imagine that once we are introduced to Jesus, he has us, and that's that. We forget that evil has no intention of permitting us to follow Jesus undisturbed. And even though God is *not* at war with us, evil is. And between it, the world, and the flesh, we are still in a war. Just not with God.

How we respond to God's peacemaking effort with us—how we become more hopeful in the presence of suffering—is to continually declare where there are any holdout parts of us. I must identify parts that contain the memory of the wounds I have sustained from others or, even more likely, from myself, that still believe that the war with God continues.

Our surrender to Jesus gives him governance over that particular subkingdom that is our life. In that jurisdiction, that kingdom, there are counties which do not yet know that the war with God is over, that in Jesus, he has declared that we are at peace.

These parts of our lives are still fighting in their own particular way, not yet aware that the war is finished. Not unlike the many stories of members of Japan's armed forces who at the end of World War II were cut off from their command units, unaware that the fighting was over. On several occasions, former commanding officers had to be brought to where the holdouts remained to officially relieve them of their duty, some decades after the war ended. Upon being given the order to stand down, they did so.[15]

They needed the presence of one whom they trusted to tell

them that the war was over and that it was good and right to put down their arms. The parts of us that still believe we are in a theater of war require nothing less than to have someone we trust usher us into a place of peace.

For this to happen, these parts of us that don't yet know the war is over must be named, not with condemnation, but with curiosity, so as to give them the chance to put down their weapons. Weapons of condemnation and fear, of shame and isolation. In this way, we systematically rid ourselves of the cancer of our war with God, the war fueled by our traumas and shame that reaches back to the Garden of Eden.

We end this war not by getting rid of these parts but by healing them. The part that carries the wound of my absent father or my critical mother. The part that carries the scar of the sexual abuse. Of my dyslexia that no one noticed but that wreaked havoc for me in school. Of my having grown up in poverty. Of my displeasure with my body's form. Of my body's failing me in so many ways. Of my child's drug abuse. Of my spouse's alcoholism. Of the affair that my spouse had. Of the affair that I had. On and on it goes.

It is in these places of remembrance of our suffering that evil will take advantage of our long-established neural networks, telling us, as Satan told Eve, that God is a tyrant who is at war with us and does not want us to become like him. Evil tries to get us to forget that we *already are* like God. We are made to be like him like no other part of creation. We hide and hide from these parts of our stories that are represented by multiple layers of neural real estate.

We hide because there are parts of us that still believe there is still a war going on with God, others, and ourselves, and we must protect these parts from being exposed and further traumatized. Unfortunately, in so doing, we must burn interpersonal and neurobiological energy to keep them hidden, to contain them and keep them quiet. As a result, this energy is then not available to us to create the artifacts of beauty and goodness that God has prepared for us to create.

Each of these territories of our wounding, of our shame, of our suffering—each part of us must be introduced to the peace of Jesus. The peace that *is* Jesus. The peace that will bring secure attachment across all the domains of our lives.

This work of attachment leads to the establishment of safety; safety that we perceive in our core despite the reality that we will continually find violence all around us, at times even within us. Who of us has not been so angry with our children that we have wanted to kill them? Who of us has never shouted, even if in our minds or under our breath, "I *hate* you!" at someone we love but who has hurt us deeply? (Or at the umpire of our child's Little League game? Who would do *that*?) Who among us has not looked upon a woman to lust after her? Who among us has not looked upon a panhandler at the intersection and disdained them, refusing to look them in the eye?

If we are securely attached to Jesus, then ultimately, we live in a safe world. This safety is predicated on being seen and soothed,[16] the necessary hard deck on which we begin to form hope. This safety makes us comfortable and confident in our own skin. It means that we have been protected from forces outside us and from within us that can do us harm—in the same way that a child, when securely attached to her parents, lives in a safe home.

This safety does not mean there will be no ruptures or injuries or mistakes. It doesn't guarantee that she won't fall from the perfect-for-climbing tree in the backyard and break her arm. And it *does* mean there will be things she may *not* do. It doesn't mean that he won't have any fights with his sister. But it does mean that when he does, he will learn to become empathic and discover how to truly apologize and seek forgiveness. It doesn't mean that she won't be infuriated with her mother for restricting her use of the device that her parents waited to give her until she was thirteen. It *does* mean that she may not scream at her mother, "I hate you!" It doesn't mean that he won't have hard choices to make when his high school friends plan on partying at one of their homes, knowing the alcohol will be easily available and his friend's parents will be away for the weekend. It doesn't mean they will like their parents when Dad and Mom decide to move the family across the country. It doesn't mean no one will be diagnosed with cancer.

It *does* mean that we will learn to restrain ourselves or say no to the impulses we have to lose our temper or have sex any way we want or gossip or refuse to delay gratification in any number of situations. It doesn't mean that everyone will enjoy, let alone perform well, in school. Or be comfortable with who they are becoming in any number of countless ways. What it *does* mean is that when, in the turbulence of life, we are securely attached, we are *ultimately* safe.

In fact, our safety is partly and significantly dependent on and grounded in the overarching work of repairing ruptures as they occur. This process also includes taking responsibility for the ruptures we have created, naming the ways we have injured someone else, and seeking forgiveness and restitution where and how necessary. This is how safety—comfort and confidence—is formed.

If we are safe, we are likely to securely launch into the world to create beauty and goodness wherever we go. We will make mistakes, and we will get our feelings hurt and hurt those of others. But even so, we know the way home, back to a place of safety, back to a place of repair, so that we can then prepare to launch out once again in security.

But this is not how we live much of life. Whether we know it or not, most of life is lived in a war zone. This would come as no surprise to the people of the small Roman outpost of Christ-followers who first read Paul's words from his letter. For us modernists, it is easy to read right past Paul's words declaring that because of Jesus we have peace with God. We understand him to be talking in theological terms only.

The notion that we live in a war zone may seem flummoxing, even contradictory to your lived experience. Though perhaps not if, at the time I am writing this, you live in Ukraine or some parts of Africa. Perhaps not if you live in a violent neighborhood or if you are a person of color living in the United States. Perhaps not if your family is one that has been exposed to a school shooting. Perhaps not if you have suffered the serious trauma of physical, sexual, or emotional abuse. Or perhaps not if you have had experiences that have left your mind in its own theater of war so that, no matter how hard you try, your life is one of dysregulation, navigating a continual undercurrent of distress that you would surely eliminate if only you could.

But even for those who read Paul's words and find the notion of living in a personally violent world to be a foreign concept, I can assure you that if you pull the curtain back—and you won't need to pull very far—you will discover that what I am saying is true. What separates you from those who know a combat zone when they see one are the layers of material—relational and experiential comfort and convenience—that protect you, that enable you to remain unaware of those unhealed parts of your life.

Some of those parts are limited to your own personal experience; some of them you have inherited both experientially and epigenetically from the family generations that have preceded you.[17] And all of those parts have neural correlates that represent them—the unhealed, grieving, broken, and relationally separated-from-God-and-from-others parts of you. For many who are reading this, the notion that *any* part of their life is at war with anyone may seem nonsensical. But it doesn't take long for us to see how much of our life lying just under the surface is engaged in an ongoing conflict.

◆　◆　◆

In the 1980s, psychologist Richard Schwartz developed a psycho-therapeutic model that he termed Internal Family Systems (IFS).[18] Recently, Alison Cook and Kimberly Miller further explored this model in the context of a biblical understanding of what it means to be human.[19] Internal Family Systems describes our inner lives as being composed of multiple different "selves."

I have my confident self, my humorous self, the part of me that is comfortable speaking before audiences, and a different part of me that is sometimes painfully shy and uncomfortable when attending a party where I know very few people. I have the part of me that feels ashamed and anxious having to engage in home improvement projects, and the part of me that feels at ease sitting in a consultation room with a patient. The part of me that is comfortable with sex. And the part of me that is totally uncomfortable with sex. You get the idea.

We are not here to explore IFS in detail, but a minimal familiarity with its basic principles can be helpful. Specifically, Schwartz proposed the idea of imagining our inner life, with our different thoughts, feelings, sensations, traits, moods, and ways of behaving, as a "family" of related yet unique "parts"—different family members, if you will. Each of these has an important role to play within that "family system" within you. Those parts function in relationship to one another; none of them exists or has a role to play on its own apart from the rest of our parts.

Psalm 42 reflects this truth in David's words, "Why, my soul, are you downcast? Why so disturbed within me? Put your hope in God, for I will yet praise him, my Savior and my God."[20] There is the part of David that is asking the question, and the part of David to whom the question is being addressed.

I would guess that it is not too difficult for us to imagine some of the parts of our own stories that play dominant roles. The part that gets irritable when we are disappointed. The part that feels lonely. Or the part that criticizes the lonely part for feeling that way, given how many friends you know you have.

There is the part of you that is really, really funny. And the part that takes great pleasure in a good wine. There is the part that has affection for your parents, and the part that is enraged with them for finding ways to continue to criticize you for not measuring up. And then the part of you that feels guilty for feeling enraged.

There is the part of you that suddenly feels like you are a young child whenever you are with your older siblings, despite the fact that you are the most effective adult in the family. And then there is the part of you that feels as confident as anyone around you as you lead your team of nurses in the trauma bay of the hospital's emergency room. Indeed, there are many parts to each of us.

And when it comes to God, we have that part of us that has experienced on occasion—more for some than for others—a loving interaction with God; and then there is the part (or parts) that believes God still isn't pleased enough, is still angry or disappointed with us. These are the parts of us that believe we are still at war with God.

What is helpful about Schwartz's model, and Cook's and Miller's application, is the tactical help provided by our being able to name, with compassion and curiosity, the different roles that various parts play rather than sweeping our entire self into a single silo.

For example, it is easy for me to say, "I am just so bad at home improvement projects." Or "I am always so angry with my father." Or "I'm terrible at meeting new people." These sweeping statements are not just things we say. They are things our brains and bodies also hear—and respond to.

What if instead we more gently and curiously inquired about that part of me that is angry with my father, wanting to meet that part and discover how old he was when he experienced the traumas with his father that have left him with so much anger, powerless to do anything about it. If we take this posture of curiosity, we are less likely to categorically shame our entire self and will instead create room to welcome multiple parts that make up who we are in order for them to be known and healed.

Moreover, in this way we can identify those particular parts of us that still believe they are at war with God, the parts that have so much more difficulty being hopeful. We can address those parts with compassion and invite them into a place where they can be seen, soothed, safe, and secure. And with each of these 4 S's, we will find ourselves more at peace and more able to hope.

But we do not find this process of peacemaking within ourselves easy, for when we or any parts of us have been at war with God for lengthy periods of time, it is difficult for us to believe that the fight has ended. When much of our lives has been committed to protecting ourselves from the God we believe has betrayed us, left us, or at the very least simply never shown up, it is not easy to create new brain-cell firing patterns—neural networks—that are durable enough to carry our experiential belief that we are loved.

This concept is exactly what we began to catch a glimpse of in the first chapter. It is those parts of our stories that are at war, that are sick, that the doctor wants to heal. And it requires our willingness to put down our own firearms of defense to allow Jesus, in the person of others of his body, to meet us where we are so that we can begin to form hope in the very places where we have been violated and out of which we have been wielding violence ourselves. But when we do and do so in an embodied fashion in the presence of vulnerable community, we begin to expand our comfort and confidence, not just in our thinking brains, but in our very bodies, in forming the hope that will not merely withstand our suffering but transform it.

Chapter Three

A WIDE PLACE
TO STAND

◆

. . . through whom we have gained access by
faith into this grace in which we now stand.
ROMANS 5:2A

There's something wrong with me."
   She had been abandoned by her father to her mother,
who, when angry enough, pushed her down a flight of stairs
more than once. On multiple other occasions, she had to withstand the demeaning yelling in which her mother berated her
intelligence and physical appearance. It was stunning—and
then again, not so—that Cora had become one of the most successful partners at her consulting firm by the age of thirty.

   Talented, unflappable, and quick with a winsome smile,
she accelerated up the corporate ladder, fueled by her superior

intellect, a will that seemed to be a force of nature, and, as it turned out, an impenetrable wall she had constructed that protected her against any true bids for emotional intimacy. A wall, incidentally, that kept her equally safeguarded from any awareness of her interior emotional life.

Her unawareness of her interior life did not mean that she was unaware of everything about her life. She was not unaware of the "facts" of her story. She could cohesively recount the moments of her brutal childhood. She was aware, in the abstract, that there was such a thing as an emotional life and that she probably had one. In fact, she could talk *about* a great many things as long as the discussion never approached what she was sensing or feeling in the room during her psycho-therapy session with me, or what was taking place between us at that very moment. In fact, the more we considered the stories of her wounds and the painful emotion contained therein, the closer we came to *her actual state of mind as she was in the room with me*, the more limited was her expression of emotion and the more physically withdrawn and closed off she became.

Cora initially came to see me because of panic attacks she had begun to experience at night, waking her from her sleep. That I was a follower of Jesus provided some degree of credibility to the process; she too was a believer and expressed that she wanted to see a practitioner who wouldn't dismiss her faith or automatically assume it to be a source of her problem. But neither did she believe that her "faith," such as it was, had anything to do with her panic. It never crossed her mind that what passed as her "religious beliefs" were protecting her from her relationship with a God with whom she was at war, albeit an undeclared one.

She did not come for help to address the multiple layers of trauma that she carried around in her *mind*—that embodied and relational process so described in the language of interpersonal neurobiology. Her assumption was, like many, that she was coming to a psychiatrist in order to diagnose her problem (her panic) and to treat it (presumably, she thought, with medication). For Cora, "There's something wrong with me" meant that her brain was not working correctly, that her panic was *the* fire that needed to be put out and doing so would indicate that her brain was back to normal.

Little did she know that her panic was merely her brain *doing exactly what it should have been doing*, given her state of mind. In all of this, Cora was most unaware of her body and how it had become the clearinghouse of her trauma. Her panic was her body's way of sending a signal, informing her that she needed help. The kind of help that she had no practice asking for or recognizing that she needed.

And indeed, for Cora to begin to imagine hope in the midst of her suffering, she needed to become aware of what her body was telling her.

◆　◆　◆

To *stand* on one's feet grounds and mobilizes a person. Developmentally, an infant may first crawl, but standing, wobbly-legged though it may be, is the first step toward . . . well, toward more steps. When you consciously pay attention to the sensations you perceive when you stand, you feel the weight of your body as it is, literally, grounded through your legs and feet. You sense stability. You are at your full height.

Moreover, you are prepared to be as quickly mobile as a human can be. Far faster, far more efficient than crawling. Yes, should you fall, more dangerous to be sure. But just watch any video of a newborn foal finding its feet. From those first, tentative movements to finding their footing on spindly legs, to walking and then running with its mother and the herd, it becomes more of its true self as it finds its legs and stands.

To stand is one way in which a growing human has greater agency in the world, as well as how that person knows where he or she "is." To be upright and steady creates confidence and comfort in one's body. Both toddlers and physically compromised adults (often due to the natural aging process) who are unsteady on their feet demonstrate a greater degree of fragility in the world for obvious reasons. To literally feel your feet, legs, hips, torso, shoulders, arms, and head as you stand provides you with a sense of subjective comfort and confidence, especially in the wake of trauma.[1]

Consider Paul's words that I referenced at the beginning of this chapter, then, beyond their metaphorical implication. Imagine that "standing" in grace—that experience of receiving from God the goodness and beauty of his own joyful self in the face of our deserving nothing of the kind—implies that we sense it in our body. We have become aware of physical comfort and confidence that are matched by an emotional sense of relief and well-being.

I am not here implying that Paul was intending his readers to imagine his words in this way. I am, however, suggesting that this is one way in which the language of Scripture points to material realities that reflect the comprehensive nature of God making all things new. Our bodies are actually part of the enterprise. Our bodies, over which we have agency, can be willed to give and receive the very grace we have received from God—not grace as limited to a theological, in-our-thoughts-only reality, but grace as we receive and pass it along in our voices, our body language, and our eye contact. This kind of grace we literally offer by keeping our temper and our tone calm and at ease when we want to yell at our children. (Not that I have ever wanted to do that.)

Again, we will not perceive something as fully "true" for us as humans until we sense it in our chests. Our encounter with it first must cross the threshold that enables us to apprehend it in our bodies—within those domains of our mind with which we *sense*, *image*, and *feel* and to which we *physically respond with actions*, no matter how subtle, as well as that domain with which we operate cognitively, with which we *think*. Until it does, we will be limited in our ability to believe. We are not yet ready to "believe"—to be living as if—it is trustworthy, true. However, these things that we *do* sense in our chests must also have language that enables us to make sense of what we are sensing.

In chapter 24 of Luke's Gospel, it was difficult for the two friends on the road to Emmaus to fully capture who Jesus was, and thereby understand what was happening, until he broke bread with them. He had been telling them many things for some time, and of course this all took place while on a walk—a physical activity.

Not until he broke bread with them were their eyes "opened." Not until their physical encounter with him crossed a mysterious—albeit necessarily material and relational— border of intimacy that included a meal and all that it entailed would they become more fully aware of his presence as he truly was.

In the breaking of bread, they did not merely have a stroke of insight into the abstract notion of "who Jesus is." One would expect that they also *sensed* and *felt in their bodies* their awareness of Jesus at a depth to which heretofore they had not—and that was contingent upon his physical act of gratitude and generosity in breaking the bread.

Then, in Jesus's vanishing, in his going, he did not truly leave them—he further drew them toward himself. He had given them a taste of what was to come, but he now wanted them to grow into people who would be fully able to tolerate that new heaven and earth when it arrived.

Notice that they did not remain in their home, basking in the light of having been with Jesus, keeping it to themselves. No, they immediately went to find the others. What they had experienced in their physicality that brought them to a fuller awareness of Jesus's presence was now continued in their actual embodied movement toward others. In this way, their bodies were once again, as in Genesis 2, a beginning place for new creation.[2]

This experience of embodied integration—the inclusion of the body as a necessary part of spiritual renewal—leads us to want to extend it to others. The creation of beauty and goodness out of carnage—the resurrected Jesus in the wake of crucifixion—opens the door to greater and greater creative acts and to the most durable formation of hope. Hope that is sustainable because it has emerged from crucifixion, from suffering.

Theologians have helpfully commented on what it was

about this particular act of Jesus that made these two disciples able to see what before they could not.[3] In a moment, all of the words that Jesus had been speaking up to and including his giving thanks for the meal combined with his action to open their eyes. Jesus's words were necessary—but his embodied engagement in the breaking of bread was no less so in order that their eyes might be opened. It required the entirety of their minds to be engaged.

In a similar way, Paul writes words that further tell the story of Jesus—"through whom we have gained access by faith into this grace in which we now stand"—words that are beautiful and necessary.[4] *And yet*, for the two friends on their way to Emmaus and for Cora, the words only became fully realized by the listeners upon their emergence in embodied fashion in real time and space. Without these actions, this physical engagement, we, like they, remain on the outer orbit of our mind's imagination and limited in the way we can understand them.

Consider, for example, Paul's phrase "... this grace in which we now stand" as Cora attempted to receive these words in a meaningful way. We may not be the first ones to have gone to war (that was the first man and woman), but war has never been far from us. For us it may have begun with our grandparents and then our parents. Or perhaps with a teacher or someone we thought was our friend. Or the man you thought you were in love with who turned out to be abusive. Or, in Cora's case, both her father and her mother.

But no matter who begins a war with us, we often turn it on ourselves in order to protect ourselves from the intimacy that has been the context of so much violence in the first place. For Cora, in order to protect herself from feeling the reservoir of pain that she held, she continued to wall it off with her intellect and her relentless pursuit of advancing in her work. Unknowingly, she disregarded the distress signals that her body had been sending since she was a young girl.

Permitting herself to sense anything in her physicality that might echo that pain or herald the oncoming wave of disintegration that she knew would follow was untenable. By disintegration, I am referring to what we mean in the language of IPNB when the different functional domains of the mind are no longer working well together, not unlike an orchestra that suddenly loses its conductor. Our sensations, images, feelings, thoughts, and bodily movements do not act together in a unified, coherent whole. They are not integrated. They are, rather, *dis-integrated*.

Hence, as Cora found herself in more disintegrated states, the notion of grace was inaccessible to her in its fullness because, in order for it to become fully real—for her to *stand* in grace in a way that was beyond metaphor—the entirety of her mind's various domains required her to sense it in her body. But that required that she open the doors to the rooms of the embodied memories of her trauma. This would allow the neural networks representing those memories to be accessed by alternative networks, networks that represented Cora's receptivity to empathy, networks that would both calm her brain stem and provide for her a novel relational and embodied experience that she could hold and practice, repeating in her memory.

She began, gradually, to be open to brief moments of reflecting on the places in her body where she noticed slight shifts in what she was sensing, even when she was talking about something pleasant. We next moved to her speaking of things that were only slightly uncomfortable emotionally: a time when she was disappointed about a grade she received in college; the sadness she felt when one of her few close friends moved to another city.

Given time and practice, she was able to "ground" or steady herself physically, emotionally, and cognitively when she began to feel somewhat shaky (literally). She expanded her capacity to recall more uncomfortable memories because she was simultaneously developing the agency to reduce her distress by attuning to it in her body and quieting it through a number of tactics, including deep breathing exercises. She was able to do this in no small part as a result of paying attention to my empathic connection with her and "borrowing" my brain's tranquility to calm her own and, by extension, her body as well.

Eventually, I referred her to a colleague of mine who led her through a course of EMDR.[5] These sessions significantly strengthened the work she had begun with me. All of this helped make the notion of grace more accessible, more embodied to Cora; it had moved from a place of abstraction in her mind and in the Bible to an embodied encounter. And the entire notion of it was reinforced when reading the words of Paul that follow "grace."

In this case, until we comprehend grace in our bodies, it will remain confined to Webster's Dictionary or a theological commentary. That we don't know it in our sensory awareness doesn't mean it does not exist, merely that we remain limited in terms of how we appropriate it in our lives. As with justification, what we call grace can be so limited to an abstraction that we do not have the opportunity to sense it—or, more accurately, we are often unaware that we are sensing it when we do.

Paul draws our attention to a *person*, to Jesus, *through whom* something has happened. And I am now drawing your attention to the language Paul uses. As I read his words, I am made aware that it is in the context of a relationship with a real, embodied person who now exists in a realm that we cannot yet see—that of heaven, at the Father's right hand—that I have an encounter in which I sense, image, and feel and to which I have a physical reaction in addition to cognitive responses. It is by the way I sense, image, feel, think, and have those embodied responses to Jesus's words *as they, too, are delivered through the interactions I have with other members of his body that my imagination can then carry them with me.*

We see in the way Paul refers to this grace something that is dependent on the presence and power of Jesus, "through whom we have gained access." We must recall that when Paul, a Jew of the Roman Empire, wrote about Jesus, he only ever understood him to be the Messiah, the King. And not just of Israel but of the entire world, the real, material world. Jesus was Lord.

Paul was not talking about a philosophy or some disembodied "spirituality." He was talking about *what was happening in history as he lived it.* And this history was centered around a particular Person. And this Person, Jesus, himself regularly and frequently cited the Tanakh (the Hebrew Bible—the Law, the Prophets, and the Writings, of which the Psalms were a part).

What has this to do with the formation of hope in the context of suffering? First, it is important to recall that it was common for Jesus, whenever he was teaching, to cite or draw from the foundational texts of his Hebrew context. He did not merely cherry-pick texts to use them to his advantage; they were not simply convenient ways for him to advance his "new way of thinking" or for him to overpower others by making the texts say what he wanted them to say. Rather, they were the fundamental ground in which the seeds of his mission germinated.

He did not merely appeal to these texts. He was their climax. He was their fulfillment. His person was the fullness of the story they were trying to tell. In fact, he *was* the story they were trying to tell.

They were all about pointing to him. Thus, it is not just which texts he appeals to (which is important in and of itself) but *that* he appeals to them that is so significant.[6] That Jesus was their fulfilment is why *we* pay attention to them.

When it comes, then, to the grace in which we stand, we can first think of Genesis 2:7, in which we are reminded that we are dust and breath. And the sequence is important. For we begin as bodies into which God breathes the breath of life. This is further developed by Paul in 1 Corinthians 12, where he explores the notion of Jesus's body being the community of his followers, a community that both individually and collectively is also inhabited by the breath of God, the Holy Spirit.

This was such a contrast to the pervading Greek and Roman culture that saw the body, yes, as beautiful, but also as something that could be used however one wanted to use it. If you were not a Roman citizen, especially if you were a slave, a citizen could demand the use of your body whenever and however (usually) he wanted.

But this was not the way of the Hebrews. For them, the body was essential to being human, part of God's good creation. The body, unlike in the cultures around them—and unlike in our culture as well—was not merely an extension of their "real" self that was comprised of feelings and thoughts, some separate outer garment that they "owned" and could do with or dispose of as they pleased. It was not primarily a burden that they had to put up with until they could reach that ideal state of which the philosopher Plato taught.

No, for the Hebrews, the body was part of the *very good* of which God spoke concerning what he had made. Moreover, the body—like the breath that infused it with life—was a *gift*. It was not something that belonged to them. It belonged to God, and as such was something beautiful to be stewarded. Hence, as Paul draws his readers' attention to this grace in which we *stand*, he intentionally employs a physical metaphor that echoes the sacredness of the body in a world that minimized it, saw it as utilitarian at best, or despised it at worst—simultaneously elevating the significance of the material world in general. We see, then, how these words that emphasize physical metaphors instruct us and carry implications beyond the immediacy of the language itself.

Furthermore, returning to Genesis 2:7, we see that the sequence of the creation of *adam* (Hebrew for "man") was important: God begins with dust and then breathes the breath of life into it. This sequence reflects the natural "sequence" in which the central nervous system works, that being, generally, bottom to top and right to left, which we briefly explored in chapter 1.[7]

Sensations are delivered to our spinal cord (the "bottom") and then ascend via neuron connections through particular tracts in the cord to the lower brain at the level of the brain stem. Those that are coming from the internal body organs in particular travel to the right hemisphere of the brain. From there, they cross to the left hemisphere to those parts of our brain where we begin to add logic and language to the entire process, eventually telling a story about ourselves and our experience of the world.

This means that, to put it succinctly, first we sense, and then we make sense of what we sense. Before we "think" about the world, we are sensing what our bodies are taking in; this input then provides what we can use to reflect upon. As such, yes, the body keeps the score, but not just because science tells us so;[8] rather, science reflects to us how God has made us to live and move and have our being, not only as individuals, but as whole communities as well.

Moreover, specific systems within the body play particular roles in the regulation of our affect, each of which is crucial to our eventual capacity to form hope in the face of suffering. We frequently are unaware of or do not attune to these systems, but once we draw our attention to them, we can, with agency, change how they are operating and thus change our emotional states. For instance, we can notice and then change the way we are breathing; when our anxiety increases, our breathing rate becomes shallow. When we slow and deepen our breathing, we reduce our anxiety.

Another example of this is the musculoskeletal system. Our fight-or-flight system literally primes our large muscle groups to become tense, ready to run away or to fight. That tension increases our sense of distress if we do not act on it. When we draw our attention to where in our body our distress is located, and we relax the musculature involved or envision a picture of our gut "releasing" the tension it holds, once again, our anxiety reduces. Once less anxious, we are more open to imagining alternative ways of being in the moment, because we are not being controlled by our lower, automatically operating brain but are, rather, being governed by our prefrontal cortex, which enables us to make in real time the choices we would rather make and not the ones that often reinforce our fear, shame, and sense of powerlessness.

These and other practices, to which we introduced Cora, enabled her to begin not only to tolerate her body but to enjoy and honor the place it held in communicating not just what she was feeling but also what she longed for. What she wanted and needed.

. She eventually found the words that enabled her to name all of those things, first in individual psychotherapy, then eventually, as everyone you will meet in this book does, in the context of a confessional community. She became attuned to her own body in such a way that she also began to notice how other people's bodies were communicating—ways that they were conveying hope or fear or shame—depending on what was happening not only within that person but between that person and someone else in the room, that someone at times being Cora.

Anytime this happened, no one was left alone. Not Cora. Not someone else in the room with whom she was interacting. Because what we were doing then—work that we do, albeit imperfectly, every time we step into community together—is the very thing that David of the Old Testament was referring to when he wrote Psalm 31.[9] This poem expresses many things. It is a song of confession of sin, a plea for help, and a shout of desperation, among other things. But it is nothing if not an ode to suffering. In verse 7, the writer notes,

> I will be glad and rejoice in your love,
>> for you saw my affliction
>> and knew the anguish of my soul.

He follows this in verse 8 with the response of,

>> You have not given me into the hands of the enemy
>> but have set my feet in a spacious place.

The poet pulls no punches when naming his suffering, his affliction, his anguish.

But then he describes God's provision in an *embodied* metaphor. "You . . . have set my feet in a spacious place." Other translations read "a wide place," "a broad place," "a safe place." Imagine for a moment a setting in which you were standing but were at risk of falling. Would you want to be on a narrow path overlooking a deep chasm? Would you want to be on a small platform atop a pole many feet above the ground? Or would you rather find yourself in a field of lush, soft grass or moss? If you need to catch or keep your balance—or should you lose it— what sort of geography do you want to find yourself in?

The picture that the author is painting is one in which God's presence *is* the wide place to stand, the place of soft landing should you stumble. The broad plain where you have plenty of room to roam around to find your sea legs and get your balance.

This is the space that is created for people within the context of a confessional community. *This* becomes the wide place to stand, as it is the embodied presence of Jesus in the power of the Holy Spirit. But it is not limited to a metaphor that is merely a theological picture of something we can't see. No. It is the very place where our bodies find their gyroscopic stability, where the spirit of God's new life is breathed into those bodies as the members of a confessional community are fully present to each other with lovingkindness, expressed in both verbal and nonverbal ways.

Our bodies are found by the breath of each other's spirits, animated as we are by the Spirit of Jesus. In this way, we are, in new-creation fashion, echoing and following the sequence of God's work in Genesis 2:7, in which the dust is found by the breath of God's life and in which man became a living being.

Likewise, the body of Christ that Paul describes in 1 Corinthians 12 is animated by the same breath of the Spirit we encounter in Genesis 2, and then later in Acts 2. And we see that the work of God, expressed in the mechanics of the interpersonal neurobiological realities, manifests as the Spirit-filled life that energizes us—his people—to begin to form hope. Hope that we must practice in the swirling seas of our suffering.

But for Cora and for many others, that work of the formation of hope must be preceded by an awareness that we live in a world, as the poet Gerard Manley Hopkins reminds us, that is shot through with the glory of God. Glory, the fullness of which we will not know until the last day but which we have already been invited to occupy. We now turn to that glory. When we pay attention to it, glory becomes *the* transforming feature of our suffering as we persevere on our road to the hope that will not put us to shame.

Chapter Four

GLORY

◆

And we boast in the hope of the glory of God.

ROMANS 5:2B

The tears streamed forth from Cheyney without measure and seemingly without end. But not without her allowing me, as best she could, to hold her gaze through the torrent. This lasted for no less than two to three minutes, which, when happening in the presence of the others in the confessional community, can seem like an eon. As the cascade slowed, I paused the process and invited her to begin to look at the faces of the others in the room who had joined me—joined her—in being fully present with her in her moment of travail.

Temperamentally sensitive, Cheyney, now in her late thirties, had been sent to a boarding school as a sixth grader, the third of four siblings born to parents who worked for an NGO in a developing country. It was in that school that she had been

55

systematically bullied by older girls for the better part of five years. She was later taken advantage of sexually by an older boy at the school whom she had turned to as an emotional haven. This led to an unwanted pregnancy that was quietly ended, facilitated by her parents who were overwhelmed by their own lives, not to mention the geographical distance between them and the school Cheyney attended.

She'd had an encounter with Jesus while at college, which was life-changing in many respects. But the residue from the bullying and the abortion haunted her, even after she married and began to have other children. It was then, as she became a mother, that the unfinished business between her and her parents from so long ago began to raise its head.

Both her father and mother had experienced painful developmental stories themselves; their sacrificial work for underserved populations was, in no small part, a way for them to protect themselves from their own traumatized pasts. Seen as heroes within their own professional community, no one would have guessed the toxicity of their family life.

That toxicity was now extending into Cheyney's marriage, parenting, and friendships, not to mention her relationship with God, toxicity that eventually led to her devolving into states of depression, even despair—despair to the point of imagining no greater consolation than for her, once asleep, to never awaken. Despair that had led her to my office in search of relief.

By the time I met her, suffering was so deeply embedded in her mind's conscious awareness that it prevented her from being able to hope in a future that was any different than her current prevailing state of mind. And although she acknowledged that her relationship with God was the most important, most grounding one in her life, it did not provide comfort, as her imagination had little access to a future in which God—at least as she imagined him—would provide the tangible relief she desperately sought.

Yet despite her despair, Cheyney had not exhausted her willingness to put one foot in front of the other in her work with me in psychotherapy, work that gradually enabled her to become more receptive to the reality that Jesus, in the presence of the Spirit, was in the room and hard at work as well. Over the course of several months, with the assistance of her courage to allow me to bear witness to her story, she readied herself to become part of a confessional community, the very community in which she now found herself looking first at me and then at others as she also permitted them to gaze upon her.

Her gaze came with an initial momentary terror of being exposed before "so many" people—eight of us; no small number when you're doing this kind of work. As she told her story of abuse, her terror soon gave way to the incredulity of experiencing the comfort and confidence of being seen in her shame and her grief—and welcomed. Not in spite of the shame and grief, but because of them.

Far earlier in our work, the notion of "the glory of God" would have made no sense to Cheyney as being the very fountain that would quench her suffering, the wellspring from which hope would emerge to transform her present moment and thereby her anticipated future. How does the notion of the glory of God have anything to do with the healing of trauma, and thus the transformation of the interpersonal and neurobiological features of that spiritual healing? What do Paul's words about the "hope of the glory of God" tell us about not merely a theologically posited reality but the material encounter with God that is possible in the real time and space we occupy?

As it turned out, it was in those minutes of weeping and gazing described above, and the ones that followed, that Cheyney was about to find out.

◆　◆　◆

The glory of God has multiple dimensions and is referred to in various contexts and ways in Scripture. In many of these passages, the writers are responding to the beauty and power and wonder of God, and the notion of our being amazed and even overwhelmed in his presence. Hans Urs von Balthasar has shed important light on this topic, not least as it applies to God's beauty and how that in and of itself draws us to his goodness and true nature.[1]

The biblical narrative reflects how the created order itself bears witness to God's glory,[2] and we read numerous instances of the writers' own expressions of the same. We hear Moses's longing to see it.[3] The Hebrews proclaim it in 1 Chronicles,[4] Isaiah,[5] and Habakkuk,[6] to mention just a few examples.

Furthermore, we are regularly encouraged and even admonished to "glorify" God. In this sense, we are to live such that all we think, say, and do is in response to and in celebration of who he is.[7] As Lesslie Newbigin reflects, "'Glory' is plainly one of the fundamental words of the Bible. It expresses that which is—so to speak—constitutive of God's being and nature, and at the same time it denotes the honor which ought to be paid to God."[8]

I have to admit, however, that as much as I understand this notion of glory in the abstract and even believe its truth in principle (not least when I have had an encounter in nature or with art in which the overwhelming beauty before me helps me more easily imagine God's glory as so much beyond it), the notion of comprehending God's glory in a way that enables me to then glorify him with my life often seems quite beyond my reach. I am so often encumbered with my own internal anxiety and ruminations or worries about the tasks I'm not accomplishing (for instance, completing this manuscript) or not doing well enough, in large or small ways, that God's glory is crowded to the edges of my mind.

Furthermore, I don't easily see how the glory Paul refers to is going to do much for my suffering, let alone Cheyney's. You would be within good reason, at first glance, to wonder what the glory of God has to do with her story of violence and shame (or yours or mine). Is this not possibly my attempt to insert a theological expression of the true nature of God into a context in which it is not intended or, at most, where it may have limited insight or practical meaning? Moreover, even if it does have a place, how was Cheyney to imagine, let alone appropriate, "God's glory" in some meaningful way as she began to walk her trail of tears in her confessional community?

These are good, reasonable questions. And I want to emphasize that I am not providing an exposition on the biblical subject of God's glory. That is beyond both my skill set and the scope of this book. I intend rather, to draw your attention to a crucial aspect of it that has immediate interpersonal, neurobiological, and spiritual implications for our lives. I want to respond to these reasonable questions by drawing your attention to a particular aspect of glory, one we typically pay less attention to but that, when we do, becomes the soil in which all lasting transformation germinates and grows into fruit, "fruit that will last"[9]—just as Cheyney was soon to discover.

By the time we get to the New Testament, we begin to see a transition in the way writers express reflections about the glory of God. They begin more frequently to reference and describe God's glory as having been made manifest in the person of Jesus. Glory in this sense, then, is not just an attribute *of* God but God in his embodied, living, breathing, pulsating presence—in Jesus.[10] Moreover, and in particular, as Newbigin again helpfully reveals, it is not just Jesus, on his own, who is the embodiment of God's glory—not, of course, that he does not in his person represent the fullness of God. But there is yet another aspect of this to which we are rarely attuned.

Newbigin reflects that it is in Jesus *in relationship with the Father* that God's glory is supremely manifested. Glory is not held merely as a quality of a single, "monad" deity[11] (much as other Near Eastern religious cultic gods were imagined). God's glory, rather, is something we witness as Jesus completely and utterly emptied himself in love and obedience to the Father, even to the point of the humiliation of crucifixion.[12]

The glory that the disciples beheld was, yes, of the Son, but "as of the only Son from the Father." In John's Gospel, then, when Jesus asks the Father to glorify him as he has glorified the Father, he is asking, in part, for the Father to *love* him even as he has *loved and obeyed* the Father.[13] Jesus asks the Father to pour out his love for him as he then in like manner returns that love to the Father.

In this case, by loving us and giving himself completely

to and for us, the world, via a path of violence, shame, and suffering, Jesus takes on sin from which we could never deliver ourselves. This war we could never stop, no matter how many peace treaties we signed.

This was the glory of God, that of the Father so loving Jesus that he then also loved us by being *with* us in our utter brokenness and suffering, without judgment, without committing violence.[14] The triune God was present *with* us in our shame and violence without directing any shame or violence *toward* us. "The glory of God is a reciprocal relationship: it is something forever freely given."[15]

Glory is what the disciples witnessed on Good Friday as God was fully present to and with Jesus, lavishing his love upon him. Jesus returned that love to his Father by joining fully with the world in his death, bringing those who are willing out the other side into resurrection.

The result declared by the author of Hebrews—"bringing many sons and daughters to glory"[16]—in part suggests we are being brought into the loving relational dynamism of the Father and the Son in the presence of the Spirit. God wants us to share *this* experience of glory. The glory that the Father offers the Son when he says, "With you I am well pleased"; and not only at his baptism[17] but also at his transfiguration as he discusses the future plans for his journey of departure, one that will include the cross with all of its attendant shame and suffering.[18] The Father on both occasions proclaims his pleasure with his Son.

This is the same form of pleasure that we long for, the form of joy that infants seek as they come into the world looking for someone looking for them. We are longing to be seen, soothed, safe, and secure.[19] At our core, we desperately long to hear—and then are so often surprised, even shocked when we do—"We're so glad to see you! We have been waiting for you! You are just who we have been looking for."

It is the weight of *this* encounter with God, the weight of *this* glory,[20] in which we sense the depth of his yearning and delight for us as we bask in that very attention and attunement. We do not often imagine, nor do we find it easy to imagine, who we would become in the presence of his gaze of joy directed at us.

But what if that was something we more frequently practiced? In this state of existence, what other response would we have but to proclaim his praise, hard as it might be to even find the words to do so, given how overwhelmed we would feel to be so deeply loved and enjoyed?

C. S. Lewis reminds us of this in his essay "The Weight of Glory":

> The promise of glory is the promise, almost incredible and only possible by the work of Christ, that some of us, that any of us who really chooses, shall actually survive that examination, shall find approval, shall please God. To please God . . . to be a real ingredient in the divine happiness . . . to be loved by God, not merely pitied, but delighted in as an artist delights in his work or a father in a son—it seems impossible, a weight or burden of glory which our thoughts can hardly sustain. But so it is.[21]

This form of glory, this fathomless, infinitely weighted glory of God's delight in us of which Lewis speaks, is a significant thread in the fabric of the glory for which Jesus prays in John 17.

It is also not the type we are used to.

We are used to glory that others, myself included, seek for themselves. I want to be famous. I want to be admired and praised for the things I say, the books I write, the care I provide for patients. I want people to think I'm important. The list is endless of the ways I seek my own glory in order to cope with my envy and the shame that gives rise to it.

I seek glory to protect myself from the parts of me that I work so hard to keep hidden. The parts of me that have survived my past traumas, only for me to find them circumventing all the addictions, all the idols I have constructed, lest when they appear and others see them, they will leave me, or as we say in our confessional communities, they will leave the room, never to return.

The notion that glory could be realized most powerfully and generatively by someone else gazing upon the carnage that is much of my life is beyond my capacity to imagine—*if* I am left to imagine it on my own. This was no less true for Cheyney, who, up to the moment she allowed me and the others to hold her gaze, only knew her trauma and her shame as the end points of her story, dead-end passages at the ends of roads that she had been traveling for years, only to find herself trapped in the neurobiological and relational darkness of the stories she had repeated about herself. In none of those dead-end passages— where she was desperate and alone in her suffering—was glory to be found.

Until now.

And so it was that Cheyney took up my invitation and began to look around the room. Everyone knew and could see the effort it took for her to shift her sight line from me to another group member, and then to another, and another, understanding the risk required for any of us to allow ourselves to be seen with compassion when we are revealing those parts of us we hate the most.

As she did so, Cheyney grew increasingly calm; her body visibly relaxed, and she exhaled deeply. As she looked around the room, people's countenances slowly transformed from compassion to smiles of delight and joy. This shift led to another transformation for Cheyney—she began to weep yet again, but for a much different reason, and from a very different state of mind. Her tears now were not ones of shame; they were tears of joy. Incredulous joy.

Mind you, the process was not without its initial accompanying feelings of perplexity and even confusion. Where and how does something like this ever happen? In what universe is one's shame met with grounded, sober, and yet utter delight? Where, in other words, do we ever have the occasion to be met with love of this kind—the kind that shouts, "We're so glad you're here!"—while standing in the detritus of our lives?

It is not uncommon for those like Cheyney, who when they meet compassion after having expected the hard parts of their stories to be met with condemnation, to find their new feeling of joy entangled with the old feelings of fear and shame. These they anticipate quite automatically and protectively as they approach deeper levels of relational intimacy. Intimacy that the community was now offering and Cheyney was working to receive.

Cheyney was being swept up into the presence of One—the one trinitarian God—who was sending, through everyone in the room, this embodied message: "We are so pleased to see you and be with you! We know your pain and the shame of those things that have happened to you—and those things you have done to yourself. And we want you to look at us looking at you, feeling only love and compassion and wanting only good things for you."

Crucially, this message was being delivered *in the very moment in which the shame that Cheyney was holding was reaching its zenith*. And because of this temporal juxtaposition, that shame was transformed. New neural networks of comfort and confidence were emerging to countermand those of shame and all that it interpersonally and neurobiologically represented for her. Her brain stem and amygdala were being quieted not just by her own right prefrontal cortex but by those of the other members of the community (along with their bodies that were transmitting those messages).

This connection assisted in calming her fight-or-flight response and helped her access her brain's social engagement system, with Cheyney "borrowing" the composure she sensed from them long enough to incorporate it into her own physically sensed experience. In this way, the members of the community were helping coregulate her distress.

Not unlike the sensation of drinking a cold glass of water when one's throat is parched, the contrast of receiving the message, "We love you and we're so glad you're here!" in the face of drowning in one's shame is like very few experiences one can have. The receiver soaks in the most available comfort and vitality imaginable while at the same time feeling overwhelmed with shame. Perhaps you have known this experience—but perhaps not.

For Cheyney, to be met with this depth of hospitality when only moments ago she had been revealing to me and the others what to her was one of the most disgust-evoking parts of her story led to sensations in her very body that became, over several minutes, breathtakingly liberating and beautiful. It was in this moment that I could reflect to Cheyney and the others that we were, in fact, tasting an aspect of the glory of which Paul writes in his letter to the Romans. An aspect that, when we practice remembering it in our sensed, imaged, felt, thought, and embodied state of mind, enables us to be even more open to our awareness of the other aspects of God's glory.

I reminded the community of other words of Paul. In Colossians 3 he writes, "For you died, and your life is now hidden with Christ in God."[22] I have often reflected on the utter beauty of these words while, truth be told, simultaneously wondering what on earth they actually mean in concrete terms. But here was an answer.

Here in this room, in real time and space, Cheyney was experiencing what it meant for her shame—and the story it told of her—to be put to death and replaced with a different story, one that was being told through the words and embodied expressions of those members of the body of Jesus who were in the room. She felt herself being held—being hidden, protected—within that community. Hidden with Christ, by his members.

In that moment, in that room, we all had a preview of what it might be like when that mystery becomes fully real. What it might be like for any of us to be hidden with Christ in God.

If it is true that we who are the body of Jesus are not that merely as metaphor—but that the metaphor speaks of the Reality that is deeper—then it is no less true that we in that body also "beheld the glory of God." Our encounter echoed the words spoken long ago, of how John and his companions "beheld his glory,"[23] glory that John could remember and record in his Gospel because he'd first had an embodied relationship with a real human in real time and space who so loved him that John couldn't help but describe himself to be "the disciple whom Jesus loved."[24]

As we in community did the hard work of expanding our imaginations, the Spirit enabled us to see a realm that we often don't. A realm in which the Holy Trinity, in the presence of this confessional community, was enabling the family of God to pour out love upon one whose embodied reality was often still (neurally and relationally) dominated by a story of violence, shame, and dis-integration. To witness peace coming to a place that had known only war.

This moment—this encounter with a hint of this aspect of God's glory—was both the result *and* the wellspring of Cheyney's work toward earned secure attachment. She moved toward practicing being receptive to others' offerings of lovingkindness in spoken words and embodied, nonverbal expressions; toward naming her griefs (with all of their attendant hurt, sorrow, powerlessness, and rage); and toward turning her attention to parts of herself, others, and God (with whom she had been at war for so many years in her narrative, emotionally if not physically) with mercy instead of violence.

This was Cheyney beginning to respond to her suffering not by pretending her pain wasn't real but by being open to the presence of others in its most excruciating, most deeply felt manifestation as it emerged in that circle of friends—none of whom were about to leave the room, to leave Cheyney alone in her suffering. It wouldn't take much for us to imagine that this was Paul's experience as well.

Thus, Paul writes of the *hope* of the glory of God, the glory that at its core reflects the loving relationship between the Father and the Son mediated by the Spirit, a triune relationship of love, of glory, into which we have been invited. We do not yet fully live in that presence. But we will. And until then, we practice forming hope in its fullness.

Cheyney did begin to *practice remembering* those moments of glory. And this practice would be the germinal seed out of which would grow—as is the case for each of us—her anticipated future. After witnessing glory like this and practicing remembering it, Cheyney finally began to anticipate a future of hope. Not only hope for a time when, as Paul writes, we will dwell in the glory of God, but hope that is given its first breath of life in the lovingkindness of the body of Jesus. A body that comforts, convicts, and commissions us as it finds us in the presence of our darkest fears, our worst sin, our seemingly unhealable traumas.

And yet, this hope is also formed by persevering in the crucible of suffering. And therein lies another mystery. For wasn't Cheyney's being struck by God's glory intended to circumvent, if not resolve, the suffering she had carried for most of her life? Shouldn't suffering be found at an ever-increasing distance in her rearview mirror? Is it not our duty to eliminate and contain suffering wherever and whenever we find it? These and other questions plague us about the human condition—what it means that we humans suffer in the many ways that we do, even in the presence of the glory of God, even as he loves us as he does.

It is to the topic of suffering, then, that we now turn and catch a glimpse of its nature and the way that hope will be formed in its shadow.

Chapter Five

SUFFERING: THE STORY OF THE PRESENT AGE

◆

Not only so, but we also glory in our sufferings . . .
ROMANS 5:3A

You don't need a psychiatrist to tell you that suffering exists, or what it is; or that it is universal, unwanted, and virtually infinite in the variety of ways it presents itself. I am assuming you have a sense of what it is, particularly in your own life, and that you know it will always be part of what it means for us to be human.

Not that knowing this makes us feel any better about it. For indeed, if God's glory is so, well, glorious, how is it that my suffering remains in its presence? What am I missing?

I don't have the first or last word on the topic. In between those first and last words (whoever *does* have them), we are left with questions as ancient as the story of Job and innumerable as grains of sand. Questions none of us, myself included, can easily answer.

What I long for is for us to be willing to approach the topic from the posture we see Paul use; and in addition, in light of discoveries in the field of interpersonal neurobiology, I hope to offer reflections that may serve to open us even more deeply to what Paul was referring when he goes on to connect suffering to the formation of hope.

By Paul's *posture*, I am not referring to his theological framework, necessary and important as it is. Neither am I attempting to provide a fully formed picture of Paul "the man."[1] My invitation, rather, is for us to consider how our immersion in the glory of God can change the assumptions we make about suffering, and not just in terms of our cognitive understanding of what we are encountering. Too often our assumptions are grounded, without our knowing it, in interpersonal, neurobiological isolation in which suffering arises and then flourishes. Evil depends on such isolation, but a deeply connected, vulnerable community can undo this. Entering community as Cheyney did made her more open to herself and her suffering as well as to others through whom her suffering was transformed. As we become more open, then, God begins to expand our imagination about how he is using our suffering to form us into people of hope— hope that will not put us to shame.

◆　◆　◆

"I can't keep doing this!" she wailed in the presence of the other members of her confessional community. "I thought that once I had figured out my story, I wouldn't have to revisit these things. But they just don't ever seem to go away!"

In the wake of all the work, why was Wendy still suffering in the way she was?

She had worked hard for many months, initially confronting an opiate addiction that had cost her more than she ever expected. From there she began to address her eating behaviors that had been a backup addiction once she no longer was trapped by her painkillers. It was there, in the early stages of her recovery work, that Wendy began to contend with an altogether different ailment, a different secret that she had kept. One that was woven through much of the fabric of what felt like her moth-eaten life.

She had remained single into her mid-thirties, but not for her lack of interest in relationships nor because she had not been pursued. In fact, she had been asked to marry on three occasions, but each time had found herself too fearful. Of what, she was initially unsure. Instead, she engaged in serial affairs with married men, some of whom indicated to her that they would leave their wives in order to marry her. Each time one of them did just that, she bolted.

She found the pursuit of and by these unavailable men intoxicating. Her anticipation of the intimacy she would experience with each of them, along with the short-lived thrill of being desired, delivered the most comforting sensation she had ever known. This became a repeating cycle that lasted for the better part of ten years. Until she met Kent.

Wendy was one year into her recovery from opiates, and six months into reframing her relationship with food, when they connected through an online dating app. Kent was single. Kent was handsome. Kent was funny and smart. He was kind and demonstrated it at every turn. He told her that the more he was around her, the more he enjoyed her presence. It was, in fact, his kindness and attunement—attunement that lacked the typical foul aroma of consumption given off by other men she had been with—that kept her from sabotaging their relationship. Not that she wasn't tempted to do so.

They went from texts to coffee to dinner to plays—and then Kent invited her to his church, the one thing Wendy didn't see coming. The one place Wendy had always wondered about but whose threshold she had never crossed. Her developmental life had been without religious exposure, and aside from a brief brush with a university campus ministry, she had little to no category for faith in her life. But to church she went, mostly out of curiosity, and also because Kent continued to demonstrate an integrity of spirit that she found to be both irresistible and terrifying. Not least when it came to sex.

Kent found Wendy to be beautiful and eventually found the right moment to tell her so. What threw her off, however, was when he did not immediately follow that with either a direct or more subtle hint that he wanted to take her to bed. In the past, that had been the usual course of action for her, and in fact, she had wondered why it hadn't happened sooner with him. It was disorienting. Somewhat frightening, even.

Sex not only had been a way for Wendy to feel wanted but also had enabled her to feel as if she had agency in her relationships. If the guy wanted sex, she could keep him, generally, as close or as distant as she felt comfortable by deciding when and where that was to happen. But how was she supposed to direct this relational play with Kent when one of the significant props that she used to direct the play wasn't *in* play?

Not surprisingly, with sex no longer a bargaining chip, Wendy became fearful that Kent was not really interested in her, that everything else he projected was merely that: a projection. She suspected that underneath the veneer of all his nobility lay something sinister. What, exactly, she had not considered that deeply. But her fear had her panicked and running for cover.

Yet instead of leaving her to her own emotional devices, Kent gently came after her. He noticed her anxiety and asked her about it. Even as she tried to avoid the question, he carefully, unflinchingly pursued it. Yet another shocker. No one had *ever* asked her about her feelings at their depths in the manner he did.

Yes, in her recovery work her sponsors had been helpful in many ways; and with them and her recovery meetings she was able to deal with the complexities of opiates and food addiction. But she had told no one about the parts of her story that had set the stage for her relational patterns as an adult.

She had told no one about her father's serial affairs. Her mother's chronic depression. Her older sister having left home at age seventeen, having no further contact with their parents. Her academic prowess that led her first as an undergraduate to the lab of a professor whom she admired. And then to his office. And then to his bedroom at his apartment off campus when his wife and children were out of town. And from there to his dismissing her when he had taken from her what he wanted.

She knew that the Percocet and the bingeing were substitutes for what she longed for; she was even aware that what she wanted was intimacy. But she had been too ashamed to talk about all the relationships that had both traumatized her and formed her shame as solidly as concrete in her soul. She had revealed certain parts of her suffering in her recovery programs. Never these parts. Not until Kent, in his unusually persistent yet gentle way, asked her to reveal them to him. And by the time she told him, he knew that he was not enough to hold all that she was carrying. Which was how she found herself in my colleague's office.

Kent himself was already part of a confessional community at our practice. And over a period of months, Wendy made her way into a separate one as well, after having done the very hard individual psychotherapy work of learning how to become hospitable to those parts of her story she hated the most.[2] In the course of that individual work, her therapist acknowledged how much Wendy had suffered. Wendy was smart. She was well aware that her life had not been easy. She knew she had made choices that led to painful consequences. She knew her shame.

But no one had looked her in the eye and named her *suffering* as such. It was as if she had been holding her breath for her entire life and was now, for the first time, given the chance to exhale. How was it that when her therapist named that she *suffered*, something else opened for her?

And it didn't end there. In her own confessional community, where she worked through her history of emotional trauma, Wendy learned how to name her griefs as well as her longings. All the while, she and Kent continued to attend his church. She met with the church's pastor. And she began to read passages from the Bible.

At some point, she surrendered to Jesus, who, as she would say later, was the one she was really looking for when she first entered her professor's lab. Jesus would help her make sense of all that she had sensed, imaged, felt, and thought. All of her story that she had been telling up until now. All, in fact, of her suffering.

But none of this was easy. In fact, there was a particular way in which her suffering was not something she could completely escape, which was surprising to her. Like many, myself included, she assumed that healing would resolve most, if not all, of her suffering, especially if God was somehow involved in the enterprise.

Yet every single step she took was difficult. Which was how she found herself that day before the other members of her confessional community sobbing with the anguish of a mother in hard labor, "I can't keep doing this!" How was it that her suffering, as much as it had been the most real thing in her life before she entered into recovery, seemed to haunt her? Even as she now excavated her life to its bedrock, all the way down to the relational traumas in which her addictions to substances, food, and relationships first emerged?

How was it that even now, as she found herself more than six months into her journey within a confessional community, in a stable relationship with Kent, and in a church family that was teaching her what home could really be like, her suffering still seemed like a wolf at her door? When she wrestled with Paul's words in Romans 5, how could she possibly imagine that glory and suffering and hope had anything to do with each other? And if they did, what difference would it make in her own life?

◆ ◆ ◆

Suffering is a defining reality of life. Just ask Cheyney, Michael, Wendy, or any of the others whose brief stories open the pages of this book. As Scott Peck reminded us more than forty years ago as he opened his classic book *The Road Less Traveled*, "Life is difficult."[3] This is as true as gravity, and it is not going away.

I don't want to believe this. In fact, I actively try *not* to believe it. I would rather avoid suffering at all costs. Moreover, I, like Wendy, have little to no category for comprehending how the glory of God that we have just explored juxtaposes with shame and interacts with it in some mysterious way to transform us into persons of beauty and goodness, notwithstanding all of the Scripture and theology offered to me about it. At first glance, God's use of suffering to change me into beauty beyond my imagination seems just plain mean. Spare me the beauty. Just spare me the suffering as well.

So I avoid this most unwelcome reality. I easily and seamlessly distract myself through the employment of my own addictive behaviors. Or, as the writers of the biblical narrative might put it, my idolatry. And let there be no doubt: I have more idols than you can shake a stick at. Mind you, I'm not proud of this. Like many of the rooms in my house that need to be decluttered so my children won't have to deal with my stuff when I'm dead, I have great intention toward ridding my soul's rooms of idols. Some days I am better at cleaning house than others. But that is another story.

It is important to know that one of the crucial roles my idols play is to protect me from suffering. Because they play this role for each of us, we are glad we have them. Who would argue with *that*? Who *wants* to suffer in any of the infinite ways that we humans do? Isn't that why Cheyney and Michael and Wendy were coming for help in the first place? Is this not why the woman with the bleeding disorder sought Jesus?[4] Who would not do whatever they could to relieve themselves of suffering? Moreover, who of us would not offer relief to someone if it would truly do them good?

All of these queries get at something. I inquire about suffering—Why does it exist? How can I make sense of it? How can I stop it?—primarily so that *I will have agency to eliminate it from my life*. But these questions—Why did my son die in Afghanistan? Why did I lose our three-year-old to cancer? Why did my business partner betray me? Why did my husband leave me and our children?—are, among other things, substitute expressions for our souls' anguished longings that we have grown weary of expressing.

One role that the questions play is to protect me from the way my suffering *actually feels*. Suffering is not just because of the pain itself but because of a phenomenon far more ancient and powerful than we realize. None of these questions actually do anything to change the reality that suffering is still going to find us. If we are alive, at some point we are going to suffer. No matter how much I attempt to avoid it—no matter how many coping strategies I develop, how many healing endeavors I undertake, or how many idols I fashion—suffering will soon find me. What are we to do?

There are many written works that beautifully, movingly, and effectively reflect the nature of suffering, our relationship to it, and practices we can cultivate to help us respond to it in meaningful ways.[5] Suffering has been depicted in music, the visual arts, plays, and movies, not to mention the biblical narrative, which is replete with it.

Suffering varies in its intensity and duration. Frequently it feels capricious, unending, and absurd: my three brothers' deaths from cancer, each one far sooner than expected; 9/11; racism. There is insufficient ink to record the array of sufferings that we humans carry, let alone their depth. What, then, is left to be said? To Wendy? To Cheyney? To Michael? The best lines have already been offered.[6]

Perhaps, though, there are some characteristics of suffering that, if we became reacquainted with them in a freshly attuned way, could potentially alter our relationship to it. In our hell-bent mission to hide from and avoid the reality of life, which means the reality of death, we avoid listening to what we have been told about suffering from the beginning. For indeed, these characteristics have been available to us for as long as God has been trying to get humans' attention.

But we often respond like the ancient Hebrews, when admonished by God:

> Stand at the crossroads and look,
>   and ask for the ancient paths,
> where the good way lies; and walk in it,
>   and find rest for your souls.
> But they said, "We will not walk in it."[7]

Instead of engaging my suffering, I turn away from it and thus, as we will soon see, I turn away from God.

I want to invite you, as I invited Wendy, to be open to these elements of suffering, curious about them, so that we can begin to connect suffering with the embodied faith, grace, and glory we have explored thus far. Along the way, our experiences will create hope in ways and places we would not expect to find it.

With that spirit of curiosity in mind, I first want us to observe and describe some of the mechanics of suffering from the perspective of interpersonal neurobiology (IPNB). From there we will also discover the categories of human experience that provide the contexts in which those mechanics operate. I intend for us to consider these features in light of the Romans 5 text that is guiding our conversation throughout.

My intention is *not* primarily to shed some new light on suffering or provide additional information in such a way that will dramatically modify our "definition" of what suffering *is*. Rather, I want to draw our attention to particular aspects of our experience that are related to hope and to how we create and maintain that hope in the very presence of suffering. Such hope will equip us to live in the real world more fully—the world in which, as Jesus said, we "will have trouble."[8]

SUFFERING OUR PAIN: ISOLATION

We tend to differentiate between pain and suffering. We use the word *pain* to refer to a physically or emotionally sensed state of discomfort. When using *suffering*, we are alluding to the endurance of pain that one undergoes over time, especially pain that is particularly, well, painful. Pain is the experience of discomfort; suffering involves the amount of time that we must endure it.

It is here that we find one of the first ways in which IPNB

speaks to what was happening for Wendy. Additionally, when immersed in the light of Paul's words in Romans 5, IPNB is intended to capture first our imaginations and then our entire lives in God's new creation of beauty and goodness. That requires a brief detour to explore the connection between discomfort (pain), time (suffering), and, perhaps surprisingly, the general phenomenon of anxiety.

One of the primal origins of our anxiety response is our neurally correlated, existential terror of abandonment.[9] I am here referring to the state of awareness we have (frequently nonconsciously but not always) that *we are being intentionally left, in direct response to our state of shamefulness.*

Such abandonment we have been contending with from the beginning, like the "alone" that God declared was not good for man and that prompted the fashioning of Eve.[10] The "alone" that perhaps emerged within Eve as a result of the serpent's accusation of God and, indirectly, of her. The "alone" that grew between Eve and Adam and then between Adam and God.

This became the "alone" that was passed on to Cain, with which he coped by violently murdering his brother. The "alone" that turned into "moving away from" through shame and trauma. The "moving away" of Eve and Adam from each other. The "moving away" from God. And the moving away of Cain from his home after he ended his brother's life.

This is an "alone," a "moving away from," whose predictable end point is death. Or hell, whichever term you would like to choose. The "moving away from" that C. S. Lewis writes about in *The Great Divorce*, where hell becomes that place where people build homes further and further apart from each other.[11]

Of course, there are multiple story lines in the Genesis

creation narrative besides that of abandonment, ones to which we are often more compelled to pay attention. The reality, nature, and role of evil and temptation. The possibility and mystery of sin. Adam and Eve's relationship to each other, to God, and to the earth over which they had been given guardianship. God's posture toward humans, who in the end do what they want to do. And so many more. All very compelling. Maybe more compelling, on the surface, than what I am asking you to pay attention to.

And I suspect that evil wants to keep it that way. For, the moment we begin to attune to the measureless power of God's desire for *withness without devouring us*—his unquenchable, fathomless longing to be with us in joyful lovingkindness and creative possibility in every moment of our existence— everything about our existence changes. It is God's longing to be with us that was no small part of why he made us in the first place.

No wonder, then, that our terror of his abandoning us is so great, given the depth and intensity of his love for us expressed in his presence. For indeed, to lose a presence of God's magnitude would be unbearable. This is what the serpent, as part of his argument, subtly and implicitly convinced Eve that God was doing—*leaving and taking his love with him.* And we have believed it ever since—to our peril.

We far too often and too greatly underestimate that our ongoing perception of our being terminally abandoned is the source of our anxiety, no matter how fleeting or continual, no matter how slight or severe that anxiety seems to be. This does not mean our anxiety is *only* about abandonment. But it is rarely, if ever, *not* about that.

So it is, then, in the face of our terror of being left by the presence of God, that we wrap ourselves with copious layers of protective emotional and behavioral coverings, just as Adam and Eve did before us, to keep that fear at bay lest we see it for what we believe it is and find ourselves undone. Ironically, these protective layers are what prevent us from imagining, let alone sensing, God's presence in the first place.

But what does this talk about isolation, about the "alone" with which we have been contending for as long as we have been on the planet, have to do with suffering—and Wendy's suffering in particular? It turns out, a great deal. What we have just explored translates into practical, real-life applications. As real and as practical for Wendy, and for you and me, as it gets.

Here's why. If we accept the idea that we were made as people whose greatest longing is to be known in the absence of shame,[12] we soon recognize that the prospect of *not* being seen, soothed, safe, and secure leads to the opposite state of affairs—the state in which we are *not* known and, as a result, are left alone in our shame.

Moreover, when we realize that the development of secure attachment includes the activation and mobilization of healthy, dynamic empathy, we become aware of how we promote the coregulation of distress. We offer our attuned *presence* to someone else who is in distress, and their attunement to our attunement—our collective *withness*—is the most effective interpersonal, neurobiological regulator.[13]

Hence, for a newborn, toddler, teenager, or thirty-five-year-old woman, distress (pain) is most potently mitigated first by attunement. This is not sufficient, but it is necessary. For any intervention that resolves pain first must begin with an awareness that that pain exists. The best trauma surgeons first must actually be *with* the patient whom they will treat, even if the patient is unconscious on the surgical table.

But Wendy had experienced very few genuine encounters with anyone attuned to her with the intention of promoting her well-being. She had little to no attunement from either of her parents. Her university professor attuned to her as a predator attunes to its prey. And the remainder of her life before she met Kent merely provided repeated reenactments of her college days.

The notion that anyone would be present with her empathically—and remain there for the purpose of walking with her into a place of healing while she sat in her grief—was not a part of her embodied experience. This crucial attention for Wendy, and for any of us, births the ability to form hope. It has a great deal to do with attention, memory, anticipation, and the neuroplasticity that ties them all together.

What we pay attention to, we remember. And what we remember becomes our anticipated future.[14] This fundamental function of how the mind works is grounded in the capacity of the brain's neural networks to wire together as they fire together, otherwise known as Hebb's axiom.[15] If I am paying a great deal of attention to my fear of being left, consciously or not I will come to "believe" and "remember" that this version my mind creates is the actual world in which I live—one in which I continually perceive that *I am being* abandoned. But the future I anticipate—the realm of the mind's activity that hope occupies—depends on what I have encoded in my memory that enables me to envision that future.

If I have limited experience, as did Wendy, of my pain being mitigated by the presence of an attuned, compassionate listener, I begin to assume that there will be no end to my pain. All I can do is try to numb it. Deny it. Distract myself from it. All the time, however, I know in my body that it is there *and will never leave.* I can guarantee you, there is little to no hope in that.

This process involves many of what IPNB calls the "nine domains of integration." These are functional domains of the mind that work in concert to enable our minds to do what they do.[16] But when it comes to suffering, two of them in particular rise to the top: the *narrative* and the *temporal* domains. We are storytellers (narrative domain), and we tell stories about our future based on our past. Suffering is, in no small part, due to the story we are telling about how our pain will never come to an end. But we do this because of the way our mind creates our perception of time.

Humans are the only creatures who are aware of our pasts and our futures in the way we are. We don't suspect that beavers are talking about last year's flood, or how long they think they are going to live based on how long their parents lived. And because we imagine our future in the way we do, we have the capacity to imagine, unlike the beavers, that the pain we now experience *will endure for the foreseeable future.* A future that we construct in our imagination based on what we are paying attention to in the present moment.

We do not tolerate being unable to know how long we will have to endure pain. Should I tell you that it will last six weeks, you may not like it, but having a deadline enables your temporal domain to drive a stake in the ground and provides comfort as you watch the calendar. Likewise, should I tell you that your pain will last the rest of your life, you *really* may not like it. But it still gives you a boundary for your mind to plot the course of your life.

However, if I tell you that I don't know how long your pain will last, your mind will have great difficulty knowing how to respond, *mostly because of the way suffering is tied to our perception of time*. Hence, even as we tell our story about how long we will be in isolation with our pain, we yet are tempted to hope it will end. Of course, when it doesn't, just like it didn't for Wendy, the suffering rolls in again onto our souls' beaches.

What this points to is the way in which our minds' temporal and narrative domains meet to construct *expectations*, a process that can contribute to our suffering. One way to describe the brain is that of it being one large anticipation machine. As you walk across the floor, you anticipate that it will hold, and you will not fall through it. You push the accelerator of the car, expecting the car to move. You greet your spouse warmly upon arriving home from work, anticipating a warm greeting in response. Most of our actions are carried out in full yet mostly nonconscious anticipation—expectation—of what will follow. And as it turns out, our ability to anticipate—to expect—is a key element of how we experience what we perceive to be suffering.

Unsurprisingly, our challenge with this ability that we have to anticipate comes when our expectations are not met. Sometimes this happens in an environment in which our expectations are reasonable, such as expecting to find bread in the grocery store. You expect your car to start. You expect your roof to keep the rain out. All very reasonable. Not that we can guarantee these outcomes, for indeed nothing is certain in the way we like to think of certainty. But these are examples of events that are *highly probable in their predictability* in everyday life, for indeed, we have a high frequency of finding bread in the grocery store.

However, over the last century, and particularly the last twenty-five years, our culture has increasingly trained us (not least through technology and use of the internet and our access to it via the supercomputers we carry in our pockets) to expect things that are, in fact, *not* reasonable to expect. Not reasonable, that is, should we desire to become mature, resilient, flexible, patient, wise people. We are trained to believe we should not have to delay gratification. We have been trained to expect to be distracted from our own thoughts by being entertained at all times—hence the need for screens at the gas pump and while standing in line at Best Buy. This is also why we become anxious when we have to pay attention to something that is not directly entertaining us for more than approximately four to seven seconds. It would be hard to believe that *War and Peace* would ever be published today.

And quite imperceptibly, our culture trains us to expect that we should not have to suffer, and that if we do for any reason we should *then* expect the environment around us to change so that we will no longer have to suffer, and that it should change as expeditiously as possible. There is little to no expectation that *suffering actually has the potential to form us into more resilient people.* This would be blasphemy against our culture's current code of conduct.

What this means is that the story I have been trained to tell myself in the isolation of my own mind—putting to use the narrative and temporal domains of integration—is that, should I endure discomfort for longer than I was anticipating and enter into suffering, this is something I should not have to do. Mind you, this is accomplished quite subtly but in every corner of my life's experience—for indeed subtlety of this nature is how evil works most effectively. What used to be helicopter parenting and is now lawn-mower parenting trains children to expect *not* to suffer, and that if you don't like the grade the professor has given you, you can threaten to sue the university. This is not unique to us in our age. We need turn no further than the first four pages of the Bible to see this. It is just that we moderns have become particularly skilled at doing everything we can to avoid not only suffering but the notion that suffering should even exist.

This is but one example of how we can come to perceive the world in such a way that we experience suffering through a combination of both what happens to us and what we do to ourselves, creating states of suffering that we believe we should not have to endure and often having little to no awareness of how we are either contributing directly to it or collaborating with evil that, wielding culture as subtly as it does, is hell-bent on devouring us.

We can also see how these two domains—the narrative and the temporal—are in play, not least when someone tries to "help" me by telling me that things will be "okay." As we have seen earlier, my perception of what is most real depends upon my being able to sense it, ultimately, in a bodily felt manner. If I do not encounter an embodied sense of actually "being okay," your telling me so will have very little capacity to change my real life. Instead, I continue to pay attention to the pain I sense, embed it into my memory, and then anticipate a future in which it will continue. In other words, I suffer.

I endure my pain, anticipating that it will continue indefinitely, unless I have a different kind of encounter with it, one in which I actually sense it being altered by the attuned presence of another, altered in a way that I am able to sense in my body. The mitigation of pain requires its reduction. But the mitigation of suffering can take place even if the pain itself does not change.

The work of James Coan at the University of Virginia has demonstrated that the *presence* of another connected relationship has the power to change the actual experience of suffering.[17] And it was Kent's presence that began to change Wendy's encounter with reality. And even though she was not aware of it at the time, it was happening by changing the narrative and temporal domains of her mind.

This powerful process highlights the role of emotion in our lives. For indeed, what my mind most anticipates about the "future" has less to do with actual events (Will I keep my job? Will my son recover from cancer? Will we have good weather on our vacation?) and more to do with what I *anticipate will be my emotional state* during those events. I am actually anticipating *feeling happy or sad or disappointed or content.* But there is more.

When it comes to suffering, I not only anticipate the emotional state I will occupy, but I also assume that *I will be alone in my distressing affect and will be powerless to change it.* Understanding this mindset is crucial, because it reveals the degree to which, in our insecure attachment styles, we do not anticipate that anyone will be coming for us, to join us and coregulate us by enabling us to be seen, soothed, safe, and secure as we long for. Rather, once again, we fear being left in the isolation where evil takes advantage and shame takes up residence. It is these features of our narrative and temporal domains of the mind in which emotion plays such a crucial role in reinforcing our perception of our suffering.

As Wendy's relationship with Kent developed, she began to offer hints of her story's shame and was shocked when he was not repulsed by it. His response gave her greater courage to reveal more. But as more and more of her story poured forth, she needed more support than Kent could offer her.

Moreover, she needed more than just tactics that a psychotherapist could offer her to mitigate her emotion. Her mind (her entire embodied, relational process) needed the opportunity to feel that she was seen, soothed, safe, and secure. She had received this assurance in many ways—from Kent, from her therapist, and now in her confessional community. What was difficult was that despite the presence, the "withness" of the others, at times she still felt the pain of the memory of her parents' departure from her, or the trauma of her affairs.

In other words, for Wendy, it was in the deepest place of her torment as she cried, "I can't keep doing this!" that the moment presented itself for her suffering to take a turn—which it did. Without attempting to address her emotional state by offering her an "answer," I instead inquired with curiosity about what she was feeling. I and the others in her community purposed to join her *in* her emotional state in order to escort her, as she was willing, into a different one.

SUFFERING: SOURCE CONTINGENCY

It can be helpful for us to acknowledge, first, that we are creatures who live our lives *contingently*. That is, we live in response to, or contingent to, the influence of the different variables we encounter. This seems straightforward. We live in a world in which our lives are impacted by other things.

What sets us apart from other animals, however, is that we are *aware* that this is the case. I do not mean that an elk is not aware that the presence of a wolf pack is going to alter his plans for grazing that afternoon. What I mean is that we have no evidence that the elk is actually thinking about their effect nor wondering about or speaking with other elk about it.

Such awareness is only one element of what makes Gary Larson's *The Far Side* comic so powerful—it draws our attention to those things that become obvious when our attention is drawn to them but of which we are mostly unaware. And when it comes to our suffering, we frequently do not pay attention to its deepest underlying sources, leaving us living more like lower mammals. Without inquiry, we remain in our suffering with no place to go with it.

When we *do* pay attention, we discover that our suffering is, generally, contingent upon three different sources. First, we suffer because of things that have happened *to* us at the hand of others' intent or circumstance. Second, we suffer because of what we have done to ourselves. And third, we suffer in the process of growth, in the effort to follow Jesus as hard as we can.

As we turn more and more directly into the light, we find that our eyes continually have to adjust to the light that is becoming ever brighter. And it turns out that naming the source(s) of our suffering is part of what enables us to take the following step in Paul's algorithm as we move closer and closer to hope.

WHAT LIFE DOES TO US

First, we suffer as a result of events over which we have little to no control. These are not difficult to identify, albeit not always ones we want to name. The sexual abuse from the family member or church leader. The jet wash from your parents' divorce that followed one or both of them having an affair. The loss of your child to cancer. The chronic illness that has crippled your life in ways you never would have imagined. You're having been given up for adoption. The accident that left your adult child permanently disabled and you overwhelmed with the isolation and silent, subtle social condescension you find yourself enduring. Your being systemically mistreated on account of your ethnicity or skin tone. The generational scourge of your grandparents' trauma that was passed on to your parents who passed it on to you. The plague of your family member's substance abuse. Your mother's or father's unfinished business that led to all that they have bequeathed to you and your siblings.

You get it. And I get that you get it. And Wendy got it.

She got that her father's affairs and her professor's abuse, along with that of the men who used her on their way to cope with their own wounds, were threads in the story of her suffering that emerged because of things that had been perpetrated against her. Processing that pain and its attendant suffering foisted upon us puts us in a tricky state of mind. On the one hand, we can so greatly focus our attention on our perceived source of distress, directing our rage, resentment, disappointment, and contempt upon it, that we do little to turn our attention in the direction of our healing. This focus then repeatedly recommits us interpersonally and neurobiologically to the very state of suffering that we are enduring, reinforcing that which we long to escape.

Wendy, for much of her life, trod this path well. Her anger and sadness were the states of mind with which she could not cope, leading her to use opiates and food to deaden her senses. The more she would recall her professor or some of the men she had slept with, the greater the burden of her emotional pain. And subsequently, the more she needed another married man and more Percocet.

On the other hand, as we begin to move in the direction of healing, evil will use the dense memory of our shame to prevent us from telling the narrative we are trying to tell. We don't want to "feel bad" by "blaming anyone," so we pretend that their actions have had no part in our suffering. As Wendy began her healing process, she initially resisted saying much about her parents, fearing that doing so was tantamount to holding them completely responsible for her life, merely a way for her to escape any personal responsibility for her actions.

Avoiding the assignment of blame will lead to a related response: our shame, which occupies so much neural real estate in our minds, reminds us that *our suffering is because of our choices—we are the essence of our suffering.* We are tempted toward the self-condemnation that holds us exclusively accountable for anything traumatic that we experienced.

As she began the healing process, Wendy would, on repeated occasions, even after several months in her confessional community, find herself returning to her story as if she were the only character in her play. "I should have known better." "If only I had never walked into my professor's office."

"What is wrong with me that I keep expecting my father to consider my feelings?" "I knew most of the men I was with were snakes—what was I thinking?"

In all these instances, Wendy was addressing things that had happened *to* her but in a way that served only to extend her suffering. Importantly, Wendy needed to properly identify those parts of her story in which things had been perpetrated upon her by others or by circumstances outside of her control. Only then could she begin to develop a proper interpersonal neurobiological response to them.

For as we will see, if we do not name those things that have happened to us, we allow the parts of our story that they represent to remain hidden. But when we do name them properly, as we will also see, we set the course for the formation of hope.

WHAT WE DO TO OURSELVES

As we have noted, pain is the immediate distress we experience as a result of a physical or psychological/emotional/relational injury. Suffering is our response to that pain over time. Wendy's father indeed was a scoundrel. Her mother's depression pulled the rug out from underneath her. But the source of her suffering was not limited to these traumatizing events.

Her *responses* to these realities also contributed to so much of her suffering. This is not to say that, as a five- or thirteen-year-old, she was solely responsible for her suffering, let alone that she could have prevented it or the events that led to it; nor does it suggest that those events were insignificant. Hardly. They were central in her suffering. In fact, her responses to her pain were Wendy doing the best she could, and she was not to be condemned for them.

That did not change the fact, however, that from an IPNB perspective, *because her responses were ones over which she perceived she had agency,* she then later regularly recalled them to memory as ones over which she now stood as prosecutor, jury, and judge. Not merely her use of opiates or her purging. Not merely her willingness to sleep with her university professor whom she knew was married or the married men who followed him. Rather, when she practiced this self-condemnation, it became easy in her mind to condemn herself seamlessly and automatically for those events over which she knew she had no agency as a young child. What was even more subtle and malignant and painful was the story she told about herself that both fueled and followed from her behavior.

What emerged was her narrative. "I'm nothing." "I'm unwantable." "My life doesn't matter." "My father doesn't see me at all." "My mother couldn't care less that I am alive." These became the running commentary in her mind that accompanied her responses to her trauma and stress.

Wendy acknowledged that these and others were the sentences that dominated the interior dialogue of her days. Moreover, she borrowed from what we learned earlier about how shame works, telling herself that it was her fault that so much of her life was, well, her life. "I knew better." "I'm smarter than that." "No one made me sleep with those men."

Here again we see the way that evil, using shame, hijacks the narrative domain of our mind to direct our attention in such a way that we construct an imagined future of hopelessness rather than its opposite, the spaciousness of hope. Evil promotes our suffering as a function of our doing things to ourselves that reinforce it.

I do not expect this to be stunningly new information for you, the reader. What is significant is the degree to which we pay so little attention to the fact that through such thoughts we become collaborators in the perpetration of our suffering. And we do this *a lot*. But we come by this practice honestly, given how isolated we often find ourselves in the privacy of our own minds.

The good news is that, as we become more aware of these behaviors, we can begin to change them and alter our relationship with suffering—discovering the crucial role it plays in our formation of hope.

LIVING IN TWO TIME ZONES— SIMULTANEOUSLY

We are living in overlapping time zones. We all know what it means to live in one time zone or another. Some people even live in metropolitan areas that are in different zones. Columbus, Georgia, for example, on the eastern side of the Chattahoochee River, is in the Eastern Time Zone. Its neighbor, Phenix City, Alabama, just across the Chattahoochee, is in the Central Time zone. But even though the metropolitan area is continuous, albeit separated by the river, no one's address is in both zones simultaneously. You live in one or the other, not both at the same time. You get the point.

But when it comes to living in this world, it is not an either-or time zone story. It's both-and.

One of the most common ways that the biblical narrative measures time is in terms of *ages*, specifically *this present age* and *the age to come*. Jesus spoke of these ages.[18] Paul wrote of them.[19] We live in the time within which the present age is passing away, while the age to come has begun with the resurrection of Jesus and is waiting for the coming of its fullness.

It is within these both-and ages—two time zones, if you will—that we dwell. Those parts of our story that represent what we are working to put to death (those parts of us that Paul would refer to as the flesh)[20] still remain, embedded as they are in our memories and in the neural networks with which they are correlated.

As much as Wendy was creating new neural networks in the work she was doing in her individual psychotherapy, and then even more so in her confessional community, there were still times in her life when those old networks would be reactivated. And she would suffer.

Herein lies yet a third way in which we suffer, one that is not fundamentally about what has happened *to* us or what we do *to* ourselves (although both of those categories are involved). Rather, this form of suffering—the felt perception of pain that is unchanging and that we must continually endure—is a direct result of new creation. The birth pangs, if you will, to which Paul alludes.

This pain, these birth pangs, no one would wish for, but in community in particular, we endure because it is a side effect of being made new. Not unlike the pain of rehabilitation of a shattered femur or of alcoholism. Or Eustace's experience of being "undressed" by Aslan in C. S. Lewis's *The Voyage of the*

Dawn Treader.[21] Or the pain of the microtears of muscle as more weight is placed on the bar of the powerlifter.

Wendy was well acquainted with the ways of suffering we have already explored. But she had little practice with, nor was she able to predict, the suffering that would come as a direct result of her pursuit of healing. She discovered soon enough that to walk into the light, to move toward integration, toward wholeness, was a painful journey that required great effort. Not unlike the man Jesus healed in John 5.

Who wouldn't want to be well after thirty-eight years of being "an invalid"? (Do not fail to notice the English word origin: *in-valid*). But now that I can walk, now that I am *valid* because of my encounter with Jesus, I have to contend with the fact that I have no job and no skills. And yet Jesus, unapologetically, finds him late in this story to warn him to discontinue his sinning. What is he to do?[22]

Or take the woman in John 8 whom Jesus protects from those who would stone her. What an unspeakable relief to be rescued. But then he tells her to go and sin no more. How is she supposed to do that? How will she feed her kids? Who is going to marry her, let alone provide for her otherwise, given her apparent recent occupation?[23]

Ask any addict who has committed to sobriety and recovery. Withdrawal from your drug of choice, be it alcohol, sex, food, materialism, politics, image—you name it—is a painful process. And that is just in the initial stages. The work of becoming like Jesus, if we are serious enough, will *necessarily* introduce us to unique suffering in that it is explicitly about choosing to live in the age to come while we still occupy this present one.

Wendy was suffering because she had been doing the hard, at times arduous, work of *not* returning to her old coping strategies. It required herculean effort for her to cut off all contact with the men she had been sleeping with, even much more so, she reported, than stopping her opiate abuse or damaging food behavior. She has been, effectively, working to live in the age to come.

Take, for instance, what happens when someone in Wendy's confessional community shares something that evokes her longing for her father's voice of affirmation or her mother's words of kindness and comfort—things that to this day have not arrived. Things that provoke the old stories that tell her she is not wanted. In those moments, she turns her attention with great effort to the comfort she receives from those in her community. And every time this happens, she not only grieves the absence of her father's and mother's love for her but also is tempted to feel ashamed that she *continues* to long for their love.

"Why do I keep longing for what I know I'll never get? I wish I could just take it in from Jesus and you all. It just keeps happening, and then all these images flood my mind of those times when I was in the arms of some man who never really wanted me, but yet I *felt* so wanted at the time. I just want to be able to love God and Kent and feel their love—and your love," Wendy said, looking at the other community members. "But it is just so hard."

Indeed, this was a different kind of suffering. It wasn't the result of something that had happened to her or of something she was doing to herself. Rather, it was the resistance she encountered upon turning to swim against a current of life that had been carrying her to disaster.

Only now, she found that the very turning revealed a weakness in her swim stroke, given how long she had been swimming in agreement with the old narrative. To swim against that current was to suffer. Suffering as one who is practicing living in the age to come, while the present age is passing away, trying to take her with it.

For Wendy, as for many others, this form of suffering included her awareness that, despite her parents' inability to offer her what she legitimately needed, she still longed for it. How often have any of us wished that we could simply stop desiring the thing we want if we know we can't get it? But with our parents in particular, the desire never stops.

Likewise, how often are we tempted to impatiently chide ourselves for not having made the personal changes we so desperately long to make? Either we no longer want to desire things that we aren't going to receive, or we want to become what we truly believe God longs for us to become. And when neither of these occur on our timetable, we suffer.

We suffer by living in the real world, one in which we are genuinely running hard after our King but are well aware of how regularly we stumble, unable to escape the realities of the present age, chased by evil wanting to devour us along with everything else.

My friends Katherine and Jay Wolf, along with the community of others with whom they work and serve in their ministry Hope Heals, know deeply what it means to be unable to escape those things of this world—whether physical, emotional, or spiritual—that continue to hound us, to haunt us, even in a context of loving community.[24] After Katherine sustained a near-fatal stroke in her mid-twenties, she and her husband,

Jay, have remained faithful to the hard work of following Jesus, along with the hard work of loving each other in the face of great suffering. They are people who know what it means to be loved deeply by God and others in the swirl of hardship.

For indeed, their journey continues to offer new forms of suffering at every turn. It is not just Katherine's physical limitations that are responsible for their travail. It is the work of being faithful to Jesus and each other when their world is throwing so much at them.

It is this feature of suffering with which Wendy was contending. Some parts of her suffering has its roots in those things that had happened *to* her, and some had its roots in what she had done *to herself.* But now, mostly, her suffering was a direct result of her turning her gaze toward the light. Toward beauty. In this way, Wendy was, in effect, sharing in Christ's sufferings[25] but doing so in the company of fellow travelers in a way that transformed the very nature of her suffering.

Lastly, it is no secret that, given that we live in these two time zones, working through our suffering will require the rest of our lives. Indeed, as we know, the Romans had any number of ways to kill people, many of which were quite expeditious. Crucifixion, on the other hand, besides its inherent way of humiliating not only the victim but those who witnessed it, involved dying in an excruciatingly prolonged fashion.

Not only does Jesus know how hard it is for us to endure our suffering—as did he—but I would also suggest that he wants us to know that we, too, now understand more of what it is like for him to be *him*. For indeed, he too longs to feel known by his sisters and brothers and not only his Father, just as you and I do. This is yet another way in which we share in Christ's sufferings.

One can imagine Jesus saying, "Now you know even more what it is like to be me—and can therefore be for the world what I am for the world. I am *with* the world—as you are to be *with* the world in its suffering, so as to eventually draw it in the direction of redemption."

This, then, is a narrative of suffering like none other that the world has to offer. Unlike the Gnostics who sought to distance themselves from the body, from the real world, in order to deny or eliminate suffering, we who follow Jesus move unflinchingly toward it, into those very places we would otherwise avoid, because we do so buoyed by the glory that we are glimpsing in the body and bodies of others who are with us. Others who, in the face of Good Friday, believe that Easter is coming.

Over the course of exploring these three ways of telling the stories of where our suffering emerges from, it is likely obvious that they do not represent distinct, impermeable containers. We may not always be able to explicitly distinguish the particular source from which our suffering emerges; it may emerge simultaneously from more than one source.

It is not ultimately crucial that we know exactly where our suffering comes from. However, being aware of our experience of its origin will be helpful as we understand how we are transformed by suffering—and how our perception of it is simultaneously transformed—as we move to the next step on our journey. For it is in the practice of perseverance that we begin to see God take advantage of the way he has made our minds for healing and for the formation of character and hope. Hope that will not put us to shame.

Chapter Six

PERSEVERANCE

◆

… because we know that suffering
produces perseverance …
ROMANS 5:3B

Anyone who suffers knows intuitively that if you're going to survive the torment you are encountering in the deepest place of your soul, you will have to persevere. You will have to endure. And don't get me wrong—I really like the *idea* of perseverance. To imagine persevering gives me the impression that I am doing the noblest of things. Who wouldn't want to be known as one who endures hard things, as one who has developed resilience in the face of continuing anguish?

The trouble for me is, when it comes right down to what is required to actually persevere, I'm really not that interested. It turns out that it seems just plain hard, and only that. I want the reward that perseverance allegedly promises; I just don't want to persevere in order to receive it.

In fact, rather than persevere, I often respond to the slightest anticipation of suffering by turning to my multitude of coping strategies that are really more like idols, or as Gerald May reminds us, addictions.[1] I know I am not alone in this. Many of us endure our suffering by numbing it. Some endure it while nursing their anger and resentment, which turn to bitterness. Some will end their lives when, in their overwhelmed state, they believe they no longer *can* endure it.

And no wonder, because—and not to beat this horse to death—to persevere requires very hard work. Hard work that is not only about changing external behaviors that have given us short-term coping strategies for our traumas, shame, and fear, but is also about retelling the stories we have believed and told about ourselves. These stories have been the nexus of the external behaviors in the first place, neurally wired in our brains as part of that process. And the neural real estate that our old stories occupy is immense, a reality to which we will return soon enough.

But somehow, Paul's experience with Jesus flies in the face of my fear of perseverance, turning it on its head. Here in his letter to the Romans, he seems to think that suffering, when in relationship with Jesus and the members of his body, leads not to collapse or denial or addiction but right onto the path of perseverance. Somehow, Jesus has become so compelling to him that Paul thinks staying in the game—persevering—is not merely something we have to put up with. No, it is in fact a key element that leads to hope, hope that I, in my anxiety, wish I could attain without the suffering, for sure, but certainly without the persevering. What is Paul getting at here that seemingly transforms his readers' despair into hope?

Different translators of this passage offer two related but different English words to express Paul's intended meaning—*endurance* and *perseverance*—whose connotations vary ever so slightly. Endurance tends to suggest durability or sustainability in the face of hardship and the resilience inherent in that process. Perseverance implies a somewhat more active posture in response to the hardship.

Both indicate continuing on our current path despite our circumstances. Paul draws our attention to how we push through in the presence of our suffering. For the convenience of our purpose here, going forward I will mostly be using the word *perseverance*, primarily to emphasize the agency it implies but also its qualities of durability and resilience.

To clarify, Paul is not suggesting that all suffering produces perseverance as a matter of course. For many, suffering is the end of the road, not the path to hope. But it is absolutely the case that hope, in its most imperishable form, is necessarily born out of suffering, even of the faintest kind.

No growth happens without pain, and growth into character and hope is no different. Perseverance provides the bridge between suffering and hope. The good news is that what we have been learning from God's good creation—in this case, interpersonal neurobiology—can support our efforts in that very endeavor.

But I must remember that, for Paul, the work of persevering begins with glory. The glory that precedes, surrounds, and follows the suffering. The glory that springs forth in the formation of a deeply secure attachment to Jesus. Attachment that emerges as a function of Paul's trust (faith) in the one (Jesus) who has come for him, with God declaring him guiltless and welcomed into his family (justified). Attachment to Jesus who, by the Spirit, has so filled Paul's awareness with himself, with God's glory. God's glorious joy in loving Paul, and Paul's joy in his awareness of the weight of that love. It is this, God's glory, that begins to create a new mind for Paul, one that he claims becomes newer and newer every day.[2]

This is not something Paul is making up as a figment of his imagination; this is no mere theological contemplation, elegant and beautiful as it is. He is compelled by Jesus himself, who knows what it means to persevere—for he did so in the presence and energy of the glory of God and the Spirit, the glory of the Father's and Son's love for each other.

This perseverance began for Jesus with his parents in their willingness to stay the course in the face of a potentially publicly humiliating pregnancy and then a flight to Egypt, both traumatizing events. It continued upon their return to the promised land, with their having to move to Nazareth to avoid the potential of more danger from the ruler who replaced Herod.

We then see Jesus, following his baptism, being urged by the Spirit into the desert to be tempted. But this would not be the only time; Luke tells us that the devil wasn't finished with Jesus, for "he left him until an opportune time."[3]

Jesus was persevering with every step he took, not least his very last. His perseverance does not merely take him *to* the cross; it takes him *through* his harrowing crucifixion. And he perseveres by joining his fellow community members who had over the centuries persevered by crying out to their God, specifically in praying Psalm 22.

The psalm is easy to misread by reading it incompletely. You may be familiar with its opening lines: "My God, my God, why have you forsaken me?"[4] But you may be less familiar with how, over the course of the poem, it takes its speakers/readers/listeners on a persevering journey that moves from agony to comfort and confidence, from being violated to being vindicated.[5]

Jesus, in praying this psalm, travels, as it were, through time—beginning by acknowledging the reality of his circumstances and his suffering. But presumably, following the course of the poem, he arrives at the midway point, then beyond to its conclusion, where it draws his attention to the confidence in God's ultimate vindication—a story that will be told to generations yet unborn. Jesus essentially prays the psalm in a way that assures him that God knows his suffering—that God is *with* him in it—and then allows him to heed the validation and hope found in its words.

In practicing being immersed in the Scriptures (as in his desert temptations, so also here with Psalm 22), Jesus can turn to them and so persevere because they draw him into the present moment of the presence of the Father in the power of the Spirit. In this way he transcends the tyranny of time that contributes so heavily to the suffering we endure.

It is *this* Jesus whom Paul has come to know—someone who does not speak to our suffering from afar but from having become intimately and fully familiar with it himself *and* who practices being attuned to his Father and the Spirit in the very presence of suffering—and so transforms it. It is this perseverance that Jesus has practiced that enables him to hope in God's deliverance and to refrain from violence, from calling on the twelve legions of angels standing at the ready, waiting for their Captain's call.[6]

Paul, then, has encountered the Jesus who truly knows what it means to persevere on the way to hope. Furthermore, we see that Paul's experience does not take place merely in the privacy of his isolated, individual self. His perseverance is nurtured and nourished in the context of the community of believers who vulnerably, even fearfully, surround him to provide the support his embodied mind requires, his mind that would eventually write this letter with such conviction.[7]

Being loved in this way—being open to the glory of God in the power of the Holy Spirit in the context of vulnerable, loving community, in the very midst of our suffering—begins to expand our imaginations about what perseverance actually looks like. Perhaps it is not, after all, about the white-knuckling effort that I fear it to be. Which would be welcome news for me—if only I could receive it. But how?

◆　◆　◆

It is important to remember that, in our modern mindsets, we tend to think and therefore read and interpret everything primarily through the lens of individualism. When I read Paul's letter to the Romans, it is easy for me to do so as if it were written to me *as an individual*. To read and hear what God is saying to *me*, to Curt, is not unhelpful; it is often necessary, and much good has and can come from it.

But this letter was written to a *community as a whole*, that at Rome. If I do *not* read it first this way, I miss that I am standing among a vulnerable group of people who are following a King they have never met—but whose reality and presence they are fully persuaded of—and doing it together.

In this communal and embodied way, they are experiencing the hints of God's glory—*not* by attempting to do so individually, each constructing their imagined version of it in the privacy of their own mind. No, in the context of community and in the presence and power of the Holy Spirit, they embody God's glory in the joy they share and in the love they display for one another. Love that is shared with others who not very long ago would have been seen as their enemies, this being a community of Jews and Gentiles. Out of that expression and experience of glory emerges their communal effort to suffer together—and so alter what it means to suffer in the first place.

I often tell people that the brain can do a great deal of hard work for a long time—as long as it doesn't have to do it by itself. Hence, Paul's reflection that suffering produces perseverance does *not* assume that each individual would have to figure out how to do that on their own. Rather, the community would, through their vulnerable life together, make perseverance a matter of practice for the community.

This practice will become as natural as breathing, produced as a natural outgrowth of their embodiment of their secure attachment to Jesus, their captivation by God's glory, and the peace with God they now experience together. This perseverance each individual will take into their life's relational interactions just as they are taking the community with them in their hearts, minds, and bodies. This reflects what

Wendy began to do over the course of her work in the confessional community.

This mindset of "I am on my own," which is far more pervasive and destructive than we realize, stands as a significant cultural structure—a principality or power, if you will—contributing to our suffering in the first place. For indeed, when I tell myself *in isolation* any part of my story where pain and shame have taken up residence, this strengthens the deeply, noxiously perceived sensation of the story as a whole.

This began with our first parents in Eden and extended to their children when Cain, consumed as he was by his shame-filled relational isolation, could no longer tolerate himself. Killing his brother Abel left one dead and the other close to dying. And in various ways, we have been doing this to others and ourselves ever since. This is the ultimate result of being on our own.

But our minds, being the embodied, relational processes that they are, were not intended to operate this way primarily. We have been introduced to a triune God who, even in our extended pain, longs for us to know his presence in the middle of it. And by his presence, he enables us to comprehend that he knows our pain even more than we know it. Hence, Good Friday.

Moreover, his presence is mediated by the Spirit through the body of Jesus—others who are with us in the middle of our pain. In fact, the absence of such a body for us is what makes perseverance so difficult— and the presence of his body, the vulnerable community of believers around us, makes perseverance not only possible but even energizing.

This does not imply that we will never experience a *sense*

of being alone in our suffering. Rather, it suggests that we are to bring that sense—of our stories with all the suffering they hold—into vulnerable communities so that we can practice revealing all that we continue to grieve *and do so repeatedly, no matter how long it takes.* And it may take a long time because of the degree to which our shame and fear—not to mention our physical wounds and limitations—are neurally embedded in our minds.

To persevere, then, is to practice, repeatedly, bringing your story of suffering into the presence of a vulnerable community that invites you to do so, and this process strengthens your capacity to persevere. I know this to be true not only from how it has happened for Wendy and many of the others you have met, but also from how it has happened for me.

A part of my narrative initially revealed itself when I was a young teenager. To put it simply, a part of me believes that I am unwantable. This part does not just believe he is unwanted by others, which puts the onus on someone else. Rather, he believes he is *unwantable*, which, in the way I tell the story, means that even if people—especially those whom I deeply desire to be close to—would *want* to want me, eventually they would see that there is something inherently malignant about me. I don't know all the details of exactly what that is or where it came from, although it's some conflation of my being uninteresting and unattractive, but once others see this cancer, I believe they will leave.

I worry, at a primal level, that to allow people to come too close will inevitably lead to their leaving. And it is the anticipated leaving that I sense in my abdomen and upper left chest that feels catastrophic. And so, without even knowing that I am doing it, I have developed ways to keep people at the very least at a slight distance. Better for me never to allow people to become too close so that I can protect myself from the experience of being left.

The result, of course, is that this part of me remains alone. Alone *and in the perpetual state of sensing that I am being left.* Which only reinforces that part of my narrative that tells me I am unwantable. You see the problem here.

Many people with whom I come into close contact might find this part of my narrative hard to imagine, partly because I have worked very hard to keep it hidden. I have worked so hard, in fact, that not until recent years was I even aware of the depth of the felt sense of shame represented by the word "unwantable," let alone that I was working so hard to hide it and to hide from it.

This story line has been like a shard of broken glass in my soul, and I have developed a number of coping strategies— idols, if you will—to numb that pain. Mind you, it did not *begin* as a story line. It did not begin with me consciously thinking as a very young boy, "I am unwantable."

As we have seen, first we sense; then we make sense of what we sense. It began, rather, as an amalgam of my temperament, my parents' unhealed wounds that they passed on to me epigenetically, and my attachment patterns that I formed with them.

They were in their mid-forties when I was born, and in 1962, to be forty-four years old and pregnant meant that you would easily be very anxious about the outcome of your pregnancy. I have a photo of my parents taken the night before I was born. You would think from that picture that they had just lost a child rather than being on the cusp of giving birth to a new one.

If you knew the details of both of my parents' stories, you would know that their lives were not ones in which they were fully seen, soothed, safe, and secure in the homes in which they grew up. They worked very hard to do the best they could as parents, and in many, many ways they parented quite effectively. They loved God and each other and sought in the best fashion to inculcate me with the same trusting faith. Anything that was good about my developmental life I can attribute to them. I have no doubt of my parents' committed love and affection for me.

At the same time, their own unhealed emotional traumas led to their passing on to me attachment wounds that left me with deficits that I was not aware of at the time, some of which I have only gradually become more cognizant of in the last decade. These include my discomfort when others are angry or anxious (I work hard to prevent that from happening) and my deep distress at the notion that I have disappointed someone—that I am a disappointment—a version, in my mind, of being unwantable.

As I reflect back on my developmental years, I tell the story that initially I perceived these wounds as feelings of discomfort in any number of negative relational interactions that involved anger, sadness, anxiety, or disappointment. If my parents recognized these emotional states in me, I have few if any memories of them helping me to learn how to coregulate them. If ever things happened between us that were unpleasant, I was left to figure out on my own what to do with those unpleasant emotions. And what I did was begin—nonconsciously—to tell the story that *I* was the source of this discomfort. *I* was the problem. With no one telling me anything different, I interpreted these moments as ones in which something about me was unwanted. Unwantable. And I needed to do something to change it.

Simultaneously, I was someone who as a child got along well with my peers; I had friends whom I liked and who liked me (although it wouldn't take much to cast doubt on my assumptions). I was athletic enough to hold my own in sports, and I was a good student. And of course, I seldom, if ever, crossed authority. To get in trouble publicly was much too shaming to consider. Many of these things were, in and of themselves, very good things, and sources of genuine joy.

At the same time, and below the radar of my awareness, these strengths also happened to protect me against that feeling of being unwantable. My friends, both socially and on the basketball court, provided enough emotional pain relief against the shard that was never too far from the surface. Doing well in school provided a genuine source of comfort and confidence, especially because of my perception of the "well done" that I would receive from my teachers. But as it turned out, I held all of this quite tenuously. Heaven forbid that I would not do well on a test or that I would discover I wasn't in the inner circle of the group of friends I usually hung out with (which eventually happened).

And then there was the matter of faith, which, quite ironically, brought my unwantability to the forefront. When I was thirteen years old, I had a life-defining encounter with God. In it, I perceived my infinite depth of sin—a word that at the time, without my knowing it, also subsumed that sense of "unwantability"—swallowed whole by the love of Jesus. And I felt it in my entire body. I realize there are many ways one could describe that experience, but I did—and I do—assume as true that Jesus's confrontation with me at that camp in West Virginia was no less real or, for me, dramatic than Jesus's confrontation with Paul on his journey to Damascus.

I immediately followed this experience by immersing myself in the New Testament for a number of months, something I had never done. I had never known such joy, such relief. I had never known such a felt sense of being seen, soothed, safe, and secure. I had never been more confident. The unwantable part of me (though I did not name it as such until quite recently) seemed to fade completely into the woodwork.

And then, unexpectedly and in a fashion that felt capricious, I was taken under by the first wave of what became an emotionally tormenting existential crisis that lasted for well over twenty years. I was tormented by the possibility that I could be wrong about all of this. All of this wonder and joy. Wrong about being loved. Wrong about Jesus. Hoodwinked by those who had guided me to Jesus in the first place. Fooled into believing that something was true when really it was a cruel hoax created by some ignorant, uneducated Middle Easterners. A story that was merely that—a story. A story which I was wrong to believe. And not wrong as in merely mistaken about a question on a math test. Rather, I was *shamefully* wrong. Wrong because I was not smart enough, not aware enough, not . . . enough.

My struggles led to the conclusion that if I *had* been enough, *someone*, for the love of God, would have helped me in this crisis. And if all of this was happening to me, didn't that simply validate that either there wasn't a God in the first place, or if there was, he was just mean? All of these worries reinforced my conviction that I was unwantable.

And there you have it. My wondering began for me as something I sensed, not something I knew as a fact. The *sensation* that led to the *making sense* captured my unwantability.

Looking back on it, I am now aware that all of this was tied up in my attachment patterns that I had developed with my parents and other significant attachment figures; but I had not yet become curious about them, let alone worked through them with the help of an outside brain. Eventually I transferred these patterns to my relationship with Jesus.

Of course, I knew none of this at the time. I responded to what I sensed by developing over the course of my life a multitude of coping strategies—idols—to bury or relieve me of that feeling of unwantability. Some of my strategies involved the breaking of every single one of the Ten Commandments in obvious ways. But just as often, and in far subtler ways, I created less obvious idols—such as my quiet, incessant self-condemnation for not being smart enough, confident enough, handy enough, fit or attractive enough, funny enough.

I have put forth no small effort in my work and relational endeavors to be enough. And while I make these efforts, I reinforce the notion that I am unwantable merely by virtue of my having to work so hard at these things in the first place.

To further complicate matters, as I moved through my life, whenever reflecting on my past seasons of emotional and cognitive torment, I would pile on great disdain. "I should have known better." "If only I'd had people in my life who would have guided me . . ." "If only I'd made different choices . . ." "What was wrong with me?"

Now, don't get me wrong—and I dare not omit this: there are other parts of me besides the part that believes I am unwantable. Many parts, in fact, that genuinely sense in my relational and embodied mind that I am loved and wanted. Parts that joyfully live the life and do the work of being a husband, a father, a friend, and a psychiatrist. That believe with all of their being that Jesus loves me and that God is for us. That imagine a new creation of goodness and beauty, the kingdom of God that is here and is coming in its fullness. These are the parts that are most real, most true to who I believe God is forming me to be. The parts that engage with people and my soul most of the time.

Most moments of the day, that part of me that believes I am unwantable does not run roughshod over these other parts. The problem presents when that part *does* show up, often in moments when I feel especially battered by fear or shame.

I share these parts of my story intending to offer my experience, limited as it is, and to shed light on at least two formidable, challenging realities of the mind with which we all contend. They are the same two interpersonal neurobiological dynamics that were pressing Wendy on that day she cried, "I can't keep doing this!" The same ones that evil will take advantage of to intensify our suffering so as to break our will to follow Jesus as closely as he is calling us to. The ones that require perseverance in the first place.

First, as I mentioned earlier, is the challenge of just how much neural real estate is taken up by that part of me that believes it is unwantable; or for Wendy, by those parts that continued to tell the story that she, too, was unworthy of being loved, with all of its furious, shaming imagery and dialogue.

I would like to think that I could simply identify that part and then permanently delete those lines from my narrative, not unlike deleting a document from my computer. The only thing remaining is emptying the trash. Just like that, I would now have more space on my soul's hard drive available to save a newer, more acceptable, more health-giving and healing document.

But that is not how it works for any of us, which is maddening. Just as it was maddening for Wendy and the others whom you have come to know in this book. This embodied reality means that our old addictions, our old longings for our idols, for our coping strategies, will never completely go away. There will always be the possibility that something will happen that may trigger a response in us that we thought we had permanently resolved—just as Wendy thought, just as I have thought so many times.

But God is not unaware of nor worried about this; he is the one who made us and knows how our brains work. He is the one who never runs out of patience or resources in his eternal, faithful effort to turn us into beings who are able to share his glory. Beings who can tolerate it when we finally meet his gaze in person, who can actually hold that gaze and return it. Moreover, when it comes to characters in the Bible, we are all in good company. This doesn't always help me feel better, but it's not nothing.

Just ask Moses, who had, I suspect, a similar dilemma. For all of the accolades that he has rightly received over the course of history, he still went to his grave with an anger problem.[8] We don't know all the nuances behind God's decision to disallow Moses from leading the people of Israel into the promised land, but we know it took place in the immediate wake of Moses striking a rock in anger rather than speaking to it with kind, firm authority. But given all the vicissitudes of his life, the fact that anger was an issue for him comes as little surprise. His life is a striking example of how we can work effectively in our lives toward integration, toward wholeness, and still have parts of us that are so deeply embedded that they continue to be sources of pain long after we have identified their presence.

Moses, upon seeing some of his fellow Hebrews being mistreated, calculatingly murdered their Egyptian tormentor and then buried the body. Later, when trying to stop an argument between two other Hebrews, he discovered that his crime was known. In fear, he fled to the wilderness, where he could then bury his grief, his shame, and his fear in his new work as a shepherd and a husband and there live a life of quiet and supposed peace.

But God had other plans, and it was in Moses's return to a life of vulnerable leadership and giftedness that his unfinished business was exposed. Following God's lead reacquainted Moses with his anger, anger that the record indicates was directed at his fellow Israelites, which would make sense.

But one might suspect that his anger also came to his rescue to defend him against his own insecurities, ones rooted in his deeply entrenched sense of abandonment and shame. Just because Moses emerged as a man who was described to be as humble as he was gifted[9] didn't mean he had worked out what it meant to be given up for adoption and reared in a home in which he was aware of his difference but perhaps unable to make sense of all that he was sensing. All that anger—directed first at the Egyptian whom he murdered, then at his own countrymen when they were fighting, and finally at the Israelites and the rock at Meribah—didn't come from nowhere.

Somehow, his unfinished business was bound to walk onto the stage. Just as King David's unfinished business would do the same a few centuries later in his tryst with Bathsheba and the murder of her husband.[10] One would think that, with all their superior spiritual capital, neither Moses nor David would have found themselves in the kind of trouble they did at the zenith of their careers. But indeed they did, potentially because of the extent to which those ancient parts of their stories, like ours, were so subtly and pervasively buried in their narratives, wired as they were into the neural networks that supported them. Networks that would not easily give up their role to newer ones just because the newer ones represented better versions of themselves.

But there is a second, redoubtable problem that makes perseverance so difficult. Not only have I practiced deeply embedding my unwantability in my neural networks—so deep that it seemingly has taken up permanent residence there. In addition, I have undertaken that entire enterprise predominantly in the privacy of my own mind, in relational isolation. In so doing, I provided the context in which shame was enabled to control that narrative from the time I was young even until now.

The degree to which my suffering persists is directly correlated to the degree to which I am alone with all of my painful sensations, images, feelings, thoughts, and perceptions of my experience of life and the overarching narrative that combines all of them together. The reason my narrative had the opportunity to take up so much brain space was because of how alone I was while telling that story, as my adolescent brain, so neuroplastically malleable, seamlessly fired and wired these thoughts into the story I was telling.

For many years, Wendy practiced telling her story about herself to herself in the dark. Even throughout recovery and after entering into her work in a confessional community and sharing her story repeatedly, in the privacy of thought, imagery, and emotion, she still felt the old pangs of shame. Then immediately would follow some form of, "I can't keep telling the group this same story. I've been working on these things long enough that they should no longer be present in my mind, let alone bothering me. The group is eventually going to grow tired of my saying the same thing over and over again."

What this internal monologue was really saying was *not* that the group couldn't tolerate her, but rather that *she* would not be able to tolerate the group leaving her when they did—as she told herself they inevitably would. Or in their case, ask *her* to leave with all of her impossible-to-bear humanity, suffused as it was not only with imperfections but, to top it off, its imperfect process of healing and regeneration. What she expressed that she believed she "couldn't keep doing" was receiving love in the face of being incompletely and imperfectly able to respond to that love all at once.

This is the form of suffering in response to which, in the face of our shame, we should not do what Judas did. Rather, we move to do what Peter did. For indeed, Peter and Judas equally betrayed Jesus. The difference, in the end, was not *what* they did. The difference was that Peter was willing to remain, was willing to return to allow Jesus to be with him in the presence of that part of him that had betrayed Jesus. Peter was able to access something that Judas was not.

We are not told all the whys and wherefores that led to their different choices. One thing we know: Peter persevered, where Judas did not. But it doesn't take much to imagine that Peter's endurance was not without its suffering. Yes, suffering because of the shame of his actions, but also suffering because of his willingness to stay the course, to remain with the disciples, to be open to Jesus, even in the memory of his betrayal of his friend.

God was obviously not unaware of Peter's struggle. Jesus was already getting out in front of what he knew Peter would do and was prayerfully cutting a pathway home for Peter before he even knew he would need one.[11] Mark's Gospel reports that the angel who met the women at the empty tomb instructed them to ensure that Peter, explicitly, was included among those with whom they shared the news that Jesus planned to meet them in Galilee.[12]

The triune God was doing everything he could to strengthen any and every effort Peter made to persevere in the wake of his offense and of what anyone would suspect to be his torment of shame. And "everything he could" included Jesus's pursuit of Peter in John 21,[13] a pursuit that reminds us that Jesus is just as interested in our perseverance as he is in our progress (if not more so), for he knows how much neural real estate has been taken up by our shame and how alone we have been in supporting that narrative.

What we see here is how Peter's perseverance was made possible because he was not doing it alone. He had friends. And in his case, friends in high places in the power of the Holy

Trinity faithfully being *with* Peter in his torment, no matter how long it took or how much work would be involved, as long as Peter was willing to be receptive to their presence. Which is how each of us learns to persevere, me not the least.

For I also have friends. Several—and they know who they are—who know all of these things about me. Together we have practiced, and will continue to practice, revealing to each other as many of the parts of ourselves as we know while being open to being searched by each other to discover those parts of us we don't. And we do this over and over again, at times in spite of my temptation to resist my friends coming to find me. For indeed, as they come, they bid me to look the glass splinter of unwantability in the eye with all of my shame and the grief from how I have so often responded to it. All too frequently I have responded by indulging in my coping strategies, my addictions, my idolatry; indulging rather than surrendering my shame to Jesus. But my friends help me to surrender to Jesus by asking me to gaze at them as they gaze at me, all as an imagined and practiced extension of Jesus and me doing the same thing.

This process, for me, for Wendy, and for all of us, necessarily includes a way of lament, something that is beyond the scope of this book to fully address. But the journey of persevering includes lamenting those things that I regret, whether my behavior or my losses, things I have done or left undone. This lament includes my naming what is real about my life and how I feel toward God in the process, with all of my longings and griefs, joys and rage, shame and confidence.

Todd Billings writes movingly about the process of lament and how it shapes who we become and the work of persevering in the face of suffering.[14] Similarly, the work of psychologist Liz

Hall suggests that lament includes the three-part process of complaint, petition, and praise,[15] all of which are core elements of the process of developing earned secure attachment. And no one knows more than she does of what it means to suffer, given her journey with breast cancer and all that accompanies that path.[16]

This practice of lament allows us to sense God acknowledging our deepest places of alienation, deepest places of loss, deepest pain—and so come to experience God's love as even deeper than we could expect or experience it to be. In this way, suffering not only nudges us into a place in which we *feel* and *sense* God's love for us but actually gives us an even more acute awareness of what it is like to be God. *And in this way, it forms us more into his image, so that we start to become like him.*

This awareness is the corrective to the lie of the serpent. We think that becoming more like God means becoming more powerful and protected from pain when in fact it is in our suffering—and in our persevering in the face of it in vulnerable community, the community of the Trinity as lived out in the body of Jesus—that we actually become more and more like God.

In many respects, inherent in the lament of perseverance is our commitment to be willing to repeatedly enter a cycle of grief. Grief that consists of naming our ancient stories and coping strategies that we then must release in order to make room for beauty and goodness.

Wendy could not release all the memories of the ache of her past as quickly as she wanted, and neither could any of the others you have met in this book. But she could, whenever those memories came to haunt her, turn her attention to those in whose delight she had come to trust. In so doing, she had to let go of the old story and its previously protective elements, elements that came with a cost, despite their short-term benefits.

Growth, then, turns out not to be about something we call progress but about becoming more comfortable being in the deepest place, being with our grief and paradoxically finding there increasing depths of joy. This is not unlike how the book of Numbers reflects God's continual faithfulness in the face of the rebellion of the tribes of Israel in the wilderness.[17]

Even those who were faithful in Israel were able to be so only because they were not alone, even when they thought they were. We need only to turn to the story of Elijah to see how easy it is for us to imagine that we are alone in our perseverance, mostly because of how our emotional states of fear and shame distort our capacity to see what is before us.[18]

Jesus—through my friends—repeatedly comes for me in his inexorably and boundlessly loving pursuit no matter how many times I resist him. And with each encounter in which my friends, in their deeply embodied ways, inform me that I am wanted and forgiven, that I am interesting and one to whom they are attracted, I am granted the opportunity to receive that love, granted the opportunity to practice telling them when I sense the glass shard moving painfully within my mind (for example, when I'm anxious about something significant that I fear will reveal my inadequacy, the inadequacy that is rooted in my being unwantable).

Then, when in response I am granted the opportunity to practice being receptive to the tones of their voices, the image of their tears and smiling faces, the felt sense of their embraces, I do not merely "feel better." No—I am changed. And the more I practice this, the more permanent the change becomes, permanent change that becomes, in essence, my character.

Practicing in this way is sometimes hard to do, given that my shame attendant continues to be hard at work, rendering its own particular form of suffering, albeit with a very different outcome from that of giving in to my addictions. For indeed, this pain leads to growth. After each of these encounters with my friends, I then must practice remembering—literally reimagining the details of the moments we have just shared.

I reflect upon and write about them in my journal daily for the next several days, bringing the details to my mind so as to create a new, increasingly durable neural network that I can call on anytime, not just when I'm feeling unwantable. I must practice it routinely for my mind to be renewed and, as we will soon see, so that I begin to anticipate a future of hope.

I am grateful that I have less proclivity toward my addictive behaviors than I had a year or even three months ago. I have realized a reduction in my penchant for envy, self-indulgence, and irritability. In general, I am less anxious about a number of things. And I am less prone to feed the demon that accuses me of my unwantability.

At the same time, I continue to grow in my awareness of areas of my life of which I was unaware even a year ago that Jesus is interested in transforming. None of this happens without a certain suffering, as we saw in the last chapter. Suffering that (at times) includes the exasperation of knowing that this practice of perseverance is one I will practice indefinitely.

For Wendy, each time she encountered a memory that would tempt her to believe that she was no more integrated than she was a month or a year ago, her confessional community would meet her in her moment of pain, her felt sense of suffering. She then would respond in that present moment by allowing herself to take in all that they were offering her. I would ask her to place her right hand over her chest and press ever so gently but firmly, then ask the rest of the group to do the same as I invited Wendy to simply take her time and gaze into the faces of those who were gazing upon her.

As she did so, she would sense the tension in her chest relax. She would sense her shallow breathing deepen. Her tears would flow easily and with decreasing self-consciousness as she saw the tears in the eyes of those who were coming to find her. Her body in general would begin to drain of its tension. And in that moment, she would know once again that she had not given in to evil's sifting of her soul but rather allowed the body of Jesus to be the wide place of Psalm 31:8 in which she could stand. And persevere.

The practice of perseverance harnesses the interpersonal neurobiological feature of the conscious domain of integration— our ability to be awake, alert, and attuned to the world and our inner lives not the least.[19] The hallmark of this domain is the role played by the process of paying attention, and the question most helpfully posed about this domain is, "How well am I paying attention to what I am paying attention to?" For indeed, we become what we pay attention to, and it takes intentional effort to direct our attention to those things that we have not practiced noting in the past.

The process of drawing Wendy's attention initially to her own body's response, then shifting her attunement to a different state of her embodied mind (placing her hand on her chest), and finally turning her attention to others (creating the opportunity for connection, accessing the energy of their empathic posture toward her) makes possible the birth of new neural-network connections in direct response to her just-moments-ago suffering.

With the repeated practice of remembering this encounter in the ensuing days and weeks, she began to develop a new, increasingly resilient neural network in which she does not just learn and remember "relief" from her pain but also learns that *she can persevere through her suffering and emerge into a wider place to stand, a place of peace, a place that hints of God's glory.*

Perseverance for Wendy implies practice—continual, repeated practice over long periods of time—that harnesses the principles of neuroplastic change, the creation and growth of new neural pathways. By attuning our attention to particular things (such as Wendy did when remembering her fellow community members' words, nonverbal expressions, and her own emotional and embodied responses to all of them), we SNAG the brain—Stimulate Neuronal Activation and Growth.[20]

For indeed, for our minds to be renewed and formed into the mind of Christ, they must practice imagining and then living into the way Jesus's mind works. This is not accomplished through magic or by some instantaneous sweep of a wand or a single revealed or discovered captivating and compelling insight. The discovery of insight and revelation is necessary—but not sufficient.

Just because I discover the secret to driving the golf ball down the center of the fairway one time does not mean I will be able to do it consistently. This is accomplished only through practice. This practice, as mentioned, harnesses the brain's capacity for neuroplastic change, creating a new neural network—like what renews Wendy's mind.

Moreover, this neuroplastic transformation requires a very long time to complete. At least longer than I would like. When a neuron is injured, at best it repairs and regrows at a rate of approximately two millimeters per day. Not exactly light speed, the rate close to which healthy neurons send signals to each other. Any changes we are looking for will necessarily require periods of time for which I have little patience.

With this awareness, we are drawn to the words of Scripture that inform us that for God a day is like a thousand years and a thousand years are like a day.[21] Trauma can upend our temporal domain of integration, that function of our mind that enables us to sense that we have a "past" and a "future"— and the movement, or passing of time, from that past to the present moment and into the future—in a way that only we humans do. When we have in our past been overwhelmed by severely painful emotion such as fear or humiliation, we can sometimes experience memories of those events and the emotion associated with them inserting themselves into our present moment unexpectedly and at times disproportionately to our present moment's circumstances; for example, when someone encounters a flashback.[22]

In less severe ways, we can "remember" in the present moment the intensity of emotional distress that took place when we were children and were powerless to protect ourselves against it as if we are still just as powerless—despite the fact that we are adults and are not in as much danger as we were when we were children. In this and other ways, the lingering memory of trauma, embedded in neural networks that have been fired repeatedly over many years, can still hijack the temporal domain in a way that contributes to our suffering. The longer our transformation requires, the more we can tend to perceive, as did Wendy, that we "can't do this anymore."

As we experience the empathic presence of others *over time*, whose intention it is to accompany us toward wholeness and integration, we find this experience makes it possible for us to keep doing the hard work of perseverance. The hard work of healing, of integration, and of beautiful new creation. It is the presence of others and their attunement to me to which I must then turn my attention—and then repeatedly practice, bringing that moment of presence and attunement to mind. In this way I re-member the event. I literally bring to mind the physically experienced moment, including as many "members" of it as I can.

In so doing, I give others the opportunity not only to be *with* me but to *take me in a direction I trust and want to go*, despite how long the journey lasts. This ushers me into a greater awareness of secure attachment and joy. With repeated practice of present moments of that joy, those moments begin to accumulate as durable memories of a joy that is the outcome of yet one more moment that at first I didn't think I could tolerate, one more moment that felt like, "I can't do this anymore!"

Yes, as did Wendy, I will still have pain and will have experiences that may on occasion reactivate its memory. But when we, by virtue of the memory domain of the mind, weave together the multiple threads of remembered moments like these ones of empathy and redirection, they eventually become a fabric and then a quilt of a neural network, one of a new story that uses my very suffering as a way to deepen my sense of being loved. These threads will form me into the image of Christ and deepen my embodied sense of his securely attached love for me. Exactly this happened for Wendy over time. As this newly developing network becomes more permanent through her perseverance—her focused, attuned practice—she more easily recalls it to memory, and it slowly becomes more of who she actually is.

As I have mentioned elsewhere, what we pay attention to repeatedly we remember, and what we remember becomes our anticipated future. And hope, being a feature of our future, becomes something that we *form* by persevering.

As we persevere in this way, even our sense of time itself—damaged by our traumas and our suffering—begins to heal. Thus, we can imagine how Jesus, praying Psalm 22, despite beginning with the agony of, "My God, my God, why have you forsaken me?" draws it to completion with confidence and vindication.[23] His "time travel," if you will, from the beginning to the end of the poem reveals his awareness of the Father and Spirit being with him, even in the midst of his agony. It is the power of that very presence that enables Jesus to refrain from calling on the twelve legions of angels standing at the ready and instead accept the suffering and separation that would bring us peace.

This is how, ultimately, we all persevere in the face of the sufferings that we carry, not least those that directly result from our turning more and more into the light of Jesus's face. And it is in this way of persevering, of enduring, in the context of vulnerable community, that we, like Paul, come to "know Christ—yes, to know the power of his resurrection and participation in his sufferings, becoming like him in his death, and so, somehow, attaining to the resurrection from the dead."[24] This "becoming like him," our being formed into his image in an increasingly durable fashion, leads to what we will next explore on our road to the hope that will not put us to shame.

Chapter Seven

CHARACTER

◆

...perseverance, character...

ROMANS 5:4A

I met her when she was seventeen, an eleventh-grade student in high school. She is now forty-five, and in many ways, it might be fair to say that Evelyn and I have grown up together. In the nearly thirty years we have known each other as patient and physician, she has demonstrated what she and others have described as nothing short of miraculous changes. Ones that, she would say, she likely never would have predicted would be possible, not only when we first met, but even after her first fifteen years in treatment.

During our time of working together, she has not been the only one to make changes. I, too, have learned things about myself, about the work I do, and about how my capacity to be helpful for Evelyn and others like her depends on my willingness to, as we like to say in our business, do my own work. For indeed, we can't give anyone what we don't have.

For to give, we first must receive, and there is nothing more difficult, no harder work for humans to do, than to be receptive to love. I am grateful for those who have been my trainers and teachers and guides—those who have stayed the course with me, who have so lavishly loved me and welcomed me into their hearts. Some of those have been my friends, whom I mentioned in the last chapter; others include my many patients, of whom Evelyn is one. One who I am grateful has allowed me to bear witness to the stunning beauty that has emerged from within her as a result of all of her suffering, her perseverance, and indeed the character that she and God together are establishing within her.

But this did not happen by the time she completed high school. Or college. Or was married. Or had her first of two children. Or lost her first husband to a freak accident. Or navigated the throes of dating as a widowed single parent. Or lost her father unexpectedly to a stroke. During all of this, she has been continually working to make sense of her developmental life, which to this day can activate old feelings of confusion and guardedness, casting Evelyn into an emotional whirlpool in which she feels she might drown. No, like all things that are durably beautiful and good, Evelyn's character has taken a long time to form.

Her story began in a chaotic home surrounded by a veneer of religiosity. A veneer that increased the difficulty she had making sense of the many emotional discrepancies she witnessed in her family. It was not that her parents were insincere in their desire to be God-followers; it was that they both had their own unhealed childhood wounds that made it difficult for them to regulate their emotions in helpful ways.

They relied on the church to tell them what was right and worked hard to follow those instructions. But when the emotional waters of their family system became choppy, they responded by doubling down on the rules of behavior that they expected each of their six children to follow. This is not a modern problem, by the way. Abraham's grandson Jacob was no stranger to his children wandering off the path, likely responding in no small part to his unfinished emotional and relational business.[1]

Unsurprisingly, as the youngest of her siblings, Evelyn tried to keep her head down and watch carefully so as to judge the safest route to take when things became frightening or barren, both of which were not uncommon. She had two siblings who dabbled in substance abuse and ran into trouble not only with their parents but with the law. This led to embarrassment for her at her church and in her school. Moreover, her parents began devoting so much energy to coping with these situations that she was left feeling isolated while also working hard not to add to the general state of disruption that so often descended upon their home.

In addition to the drug abuse, one of her older sisters, when overwhelmed or unhappy, somehow decided to use Evelyn as an emotional punching bag. She would criticize and belittle Evelyn; she would, as Evelyn entered adolescence, "borrow" Evelyn's clothes without asking, with the clothing on occasion magically disappearing.

None of Evelyn's complaints to her mother about these things seemed to reach her mother's ear. Her response to Evelyn was one that communicated something akin to, "Can't you see that we have bigger problems here? And besides, you know how sensitive your sister is. You are just so much more capable than she is to handle these things. Just be patient."

Not surprisingly, Evelyn took solace in her books, and as you can imagine, no small amount of solace was needed. It was to fiction that she turned to distract herself from her real life. She devoured Tolstoy and Updike and Tolkien and Hugo. She listened to Verdi and Puccini. They protected her as best they could from her family. And from herself. But by the time she reached my office, she was depressed and unable to rouse herself to get to school.

Almost out of nowhere—as her parents would tell the story—their once confident, she-doesn't-give-us-any-trouble daughter was making her own demands on their emotional capital. Capital that was running close to bankruptcy, and the way they responded was to ask for help for *her*—a very reasonable and wise choice. The problem was that they were not willing to do the work of their own that would be necessary to create the optimal space—the wide place for Evelyn to stand—that she needed in order to recover.

Thus, despite Evelyn's commitment to begin to make sense of her narrative at the young age of seventeen, neither her parents nor her siblings have ever been willing to do the same. And so, the journey out of her depression was also a journey out of her family system, one of fits and starts, one that has required various retracings of parts of her story over the course of the time we have known each other. It was, for her, not just a matter of pushing against her own demons or even those of her family. It felt like she was pushing against the earth.

Yet multiple streams of healing have contributed to the development of her character, the durable, reliable person she is: her work addressing her inner and outer lives of her longings and griefs; her marriage to a loving, devoted husband—along with her tragic loss of him; the births and lives of her children; her friendships; her worshiping community at her local Orthodox parish; her spiritual practices of prayer and study; and, not least, her journey in a confessional community.

This work has not been easy, seamless, or of a straight-line trajectory. Her early days in psychotherapy as a teenager and then into young adulthood required her willingness to be patient with herself, given that she felt so desperate for change, not to mention the gravitational pull of the system she was trying to extract herself from. All of this in the context of a world that over her lifetime has become increasingly committed to training her—training all of us—to believe that we should never have to delay gratification and that we should never have to suffer, training us to become less tolerant of distress and thereby less resilient. Not to mention how the internet is also certainly training us to be more distractible and therefore more anxious when we are compelled to pay attention to things we find relatively less entertaining or even distressing[2]—such as our children. Or the predictable, mundane domains of our lives. Or our grief.

As Evelyn has matured—from adolescent to young adult to married mother and then to a young, widowed mother of two—she continues to face changes and pressures that require more effort on her part to focus her attention on developing an earned secure attachment. Some of those pressures have been cultural (such as to achieve and consume to prove her worth), but none has been more potent than the pressure she feels on occasion from the system of her family of origin. More than anything else, it continues to attempt to wrap its tentacles around her, striving to involve her in its unhealthy dynamics. It is against these very dynamics that she works heroically to place more effective boundaries.

There have been moments when she could only imagine the relief she would feel—and thought that she would be so much better off, as perhaps would be her children—if she just didn't wake up the next morning, especially in the weeks and months following her husband's death. However, this work of art that is her life is one of nearly unbearable beauty—as a direct result of her suffering and perseverance.

Her life has been so transformed, the changes would be hard to believe had we not all been in the room to witness the change that came over her over the course of many months. The shift away from the automatic tendency toward self-condemnation. The expanded capacity to tolerate difficult emotions as they appeared during our time together. The increased ability to disregard a family member's criticism over the smallest of things.

For this to happen required the perseverance we have been exploring. Moreover, it is this perseverance under the weight of her suffering—in the presence of her confessional community and others—that has led to character, character that is grounded in the fundamental work that she has done in response to and in the presence and power of the Holy Spirit, who, by animating those in her confessional community (the body of Jesus), included them as co-laborers in the work.

◆ ◆ ◆

The word *character* suggests the totality of the enduring *characteristics of one's personhood*. We are speaking of the degree to which any one of us is predictably and consistently kind, harsh, easily irritated, patient, moody, thoughtful, mindless, trustworthy, unreliable—features that describe how we, in most instances, comport ourselves in the world.

In psychological parlance, the term *character* is likewise used to refer to those traits of a person that tend to be long-lasting, seemingly permanent (although not always understood to be absolutely unchangeable). The word is sometimes interchanged with *personality*, the two words being used subtly differently, depending on the literature you read.

The Greek word that Paul uses for "character" in Romans 5 is *dokimē. Dokimē* refers to metal that has been purged of all impurities, such as sterling silver. It connotes a sense of purity, purity that has emerged alongside a strong, resilient durability.[3] Paul uses this word to refer not only to the general notion of a person's enduring traits but additionally and explicitly to the type of character that one would expect to emerge within a follower of Jesus in the community of his body.

But our character is not something static, like a marble sculpture that, once carved, remains unchanging. Rather, character is *continually being formed by what we are practicing becoming at any given moment in time*. This is how perseverance, via neuroplastic repetition, leads to the formation of character; hence, what we pay attention to, we practice, and what we practice, we become—becomes our character. If we are practicing for heaven, then our attention is directed toward the development of secure attachment and the formation and bearing of the fruit of the Spirit—namely, love, joy, peace, patience, kindness, goodness, faithfulness, gentleness, and self-control.

But these fruits do not suddenly or magically appear on the tree. The tree needs tending— long years of it. And tending involves nourishing the tree, pruning the tree, and allowing for the tree to undergo non-catastrophic hardship in order for it to develop durability that will further enable it to produce fruit. Fruit that will last.[4]

Over many years, Evelyn revisited her story in ever-maturing ways and persevered through the suffering that newly emerging events and the implicit memories they evoked would toss in her path. In so enduring, her character became a work of art.

There are multiple resources that work to form us into the image of Jesus, to shape our character into his likeness.[5] We begin, of course, with our local congregations in which we worship God and take sustenance from the Word and sacraments and then are regularly commissioned and sent forth to be the gospel in our respective worlds.[6] It is in these places that we discover that the taking in of the words and teachings of the Scriptures, along with the sacraments, is a way for us to be continually reminded that life is about our having a choice between two trees—the tree of life, where God is in charge of what is good and evil; and the tree of knowledge, where I decide what is good and evil so that I can get what I want at the expense of others.[7] Taking in Scripture and becoming increasingly filled with God's wisdom in everything I do reflects the better choice rather than merely allowing myself to be a rule-follower.

My life in the presence of the people of God is intended to make me a person of character. A person whose character knows the difference between keeping the law that says I must not murder and knowing the wisdom that calling my brother an idiot is how murder really begins. The role of the body of Jesus is much more about who I am becoming than it is about making sure I'm doing everything the right way and in the right order.[8]

Additionally, in our day, there are ministries and organizations apart from formally gathered church bodies, including the confessional communities we have been speaking of here and elsewhere, that are committed to the proclamation of the good news of Jesus and to Christian spiritual formation. The principles of such parachurch organizations intend to form their participants into the image of the King.[9]

Furthermore, we have access to much written material devoted to the same purpose, all of which supports our spiritual formation through our study of Scripture and the reading of and reflecting upon trustworthy devotional and formational literature. Practices such as prayer, meditation, confession, spiritual direction and discipleship, fasting, and service. Each of these practices individually and collectively—not unlike multiple exercises and workout machines in the gym—prepares us to step onto the playing field of life to create beauty and goodness wherever we go.

The mind mediates each of these character-forming endeavors through its features of sensing, imaging, feeling, thinking, and expressing embodied activity within the nine domains of integration as we describe them in the language and principles of interpersonal neurobiology, of God's good material creation.

For example, *sensing* our being loved—not merely "knowing" that I am loved as a fact—is necessary for our character development. But "sensing our being loved" is also something that can be described as a set of interpersonal, neurophysiologically mediated interactions that involve nonverbal as well as verbal cues to which we respond.

When Evelyn first joined a confessional community, she had previously had the experience of feeling loved by me and others. But to have this same experience in the context of an entire group at the same time *with intention* was different; it was at times as overwhelming as it was comforting. But pointing out the actual, incremental physically mediated interactions between Evelyn and the others in the room enabled her to learn to tolerate them, practice remembering them explicitly, and also put them into practice in the group intentionally. This, in effect, became a spiritual discipline for her.

This way of attuning to the mechanics of the spiritually formational dynamics that are taking place in real time and space is the warp and woof of how IPNB works. It supports and strengthens our ability to live securely attached to Jesus. IPNB also enables us to imagine and thereby live deeply in response to and into God's glory (if only in the beginning stages of what that means) and to endure and persevere through suffering, so as to develop character out of which our hope is constructed.

Another element of character formation that requires perseverance takes advantage of how we have been created as creatures of rhythm. We have rhythms to our cardiac and pulmonary functions, we walk with a rhythmic gait, and we even have a rhythm to our relational interactions: we move from connection with others to periods of solitude and back again, each supporting and in need of the other.

We have also learned that, in order for someone to absorb something deeply, a particular rhythm can maximize that absorption. First, we want them to encounter an experience and then pause to pan the camera out, so to speak, to draw their attention to what they have just experienced so they can take it in even more fully and memorably.

For example, one time a member of the confessional community expressed his anger on Evelyn's behalf after hearing yet another story of how her family of origin was working to keep her in its clutches. Evelyn at first expressed how surprised and unsettled she felt; but a moment later, she went on to describe her relief and how deeply protected she felt by someone who understood her so well. It was at that point that my colleague paused the conversation.

The group's facilitator asked Evelyn to reflect on what had just happened, to rewind the tape of the past few minutes and observe the events once again, and to pay even closer attention to the process that had just taken place. This provided Evelyn with the opportunity not just to have an experience of empathy but to *recall it and even more deeply embed it in her memory.* The rhythm of this encounter began with Evelyn first having the experience; then the pendulum swung in the other direction when we gave her the opportunity to reflect on that very experience.

In confessional communities, this back-and-forth rhythm— encounter followed by a pause to pay explicit attention to that encounter—provides the effect of increasing states of integration, of wholeness. Practically speaking, we first experience things, and then we talk about what we have experienced, much like the way good parenting works—and those who are parents know just how much perseverance is involved in that endeavor!

First, our children engage the world, and then we interpret the world for them in developmentally appropriate ways. Likewise, in confessional communities, we regularly and rhythmically, in the wake of a significant moment of interchange, reflect to the group members what has just happened and then explicitly bind the experience to a particular element of spiritual formation. For example, I might say, "I want to pause us for a moment and remember what we have just done here and what our intention is throughout our process. As reflected in Paul's words to the church at Ephesus, in our work we are practicing what it means to '[speak] the truth in love, [such that] we will grow to become in every respect the mature body of him who is the head, that is, Christ. From him the whole body, joined and held together by every supporting ligament, grows and builds itself up in love, as each part does its work.'"[10]

We do the work; we then pause and notice the work we have been and are doing and thus embed the work more fully into who we are becoming—literally, neurobiologically. In the dialect of IPNB, this growth and building up is represented by the notion of integration, the linkage of differentiated parts that leads to an increasingly complex system, the evidence of which is the degree to which the system is becoming gradually more flexible, adaptive, coherent, energized, and stable (FACES).[11]

We encourage the members to regularly reflect on these attributes of FACES not so much to keep a scorecard but rather as a means to cognitively capture what is taking place at any given time and so continue to practice it with intention. These new attributes then serve as signposts of who they long to become and what they can turn their attention to in times of distress. Along the way, we remind each other that none of this is easy, that it all takes perseverance, and that it is leading us to becoming like Jesus.[12] And out of this character grows the byproduct of hope.

An example of this is the following. On occasion, Evelyn would find herself feeling overwhelmed in the confessional community, as her mind rehearsed old narratives accusing her of not having changed a whit (not unlike Wendy in previous chapters), her body becoming dysregulated with an uptick in her heart and breathing rate along with a tightening in her chest. In those instances, either I, my colleague, or one of the other members would help her examine these responses. Gently and with curiosity, we would invite her to pause, notice what she was feeling, especially in her body, and then name the story that she was currently telling herself.

We would then, ideally, join her empathically before next inviting her to turn her attention to one or more of us and to what she was aware we were sensing and feeling—and then to take that in over the next one to two minutes. In so doing, not only would her bodily responses become calm, but her accusatory thoughts would recede to the background, following her body's lead. She would regain a sense of comfort and confidence, having moved from a place of instability to one of stability.

But her finding a wide place to stand was not the end of the process. We would next pause the process and invite her to reflect on and more intentionally take in the memory of what had just taken place. She was then encouraged to journal about the experience later and bring it to mind so that it would take up greater and greater space in her brain and in her mind. In doing this recounting, she was following the words of Moses, who admonished the Hebrews to remember the Lord their God upon entering the land of Canaan.[13]

This practice portrays how character is being formed as Evelyn allows herself to be loved *in those moments in which her less favorable personal characteristics are on display*. Evelyn's willingness to continually and vulnerably be present in the group means, as it does for everyone, that the parts that "need the doctor"—the parts that are the least like Jesus—are the parts that eventually, inevitably reveal themselves and make themselves open and receptive to love. Moreover, it is paying attention to the rhythm of these encounters and then observing the experience that strengthens this process.

In terms of IPNB, Evelyn makes possible the maturational development of various domains of her mind (her awareness of her very awareness, of her body, and of her state of mind, to name but three). Using the assistance of the community, she links them together, leading to integration and an increased sense of being a person of greater FACES. As we bring these things to her attention, using this language and metaphor and linking them to Paul's words, we as a community are doing the very thing on a larger, communal scale that Evelyn is doing in her own mind.

We pause to notice and name this process as well that works to create more durable character in each of us—even those of us who are the therapists in the room. This challenging process provides the opportunity for those parts that are initially more frightened of being receptive to love and hospitality to practice becoming more so in order for them to be renovated and recommissioned.

In this way, the Holy Spirit enables growth as he uses the material that God has created and put into place for that very purpose. I and others drew Evelyn's attunement to the dynamics of these mechanics (her attention, bodily sensations, emotions, thoughts, the story she was telling, etc.), as we do for all whom we seek to help.

We do so not merely by naming and noting them as a list of "abstract things to know and be aware of *as facts*." We also point to them as evidence of what is actually happening in real embodied time and space in the context—the ongoing conversations and interpersonal dynamics—of the confessional community's interactions. By drawing Evelyn's and her fellow group members' attention to "what is happening in the room," we enabled them to look for and take advantage of these dynamics as a means of persevering in the face of all their sufferings, forming character against the backdrop of the echoes of God's glory.

This effort of paying attention to "what is happening in the room" supports the formation of character. In moments of perseverance in the presence of suffering, the degree to which we are paying attention in this way will shape the type of character that is formed, one moving either toward integration and wholeness or else away from it, allowing character to dis-integrate. The only shift is which room we are in and the people who are in it with us, whether our families, our coworkers, our fellow church members, or the driver who cuts me off in traffic.

We become what we practice paying attention to, and paying attention to the mechanics of *how* God is forming us *in any given moment* is a significant step toward co-laboring with him in that formational process. Hence, one way that we can deepen character through perseverance is to pay attention to these mechanics as we are immersed in them. In the same way we learn any skill—by paying attention to the explicit details of what is required, whether to drive a car, play the piano, or pilot a sailboat—we form our character.

◆ ◆ ◆

Character formation of course involves many variables, not all of which we can cover here. However, one framework by which it can be made a bit more accessible is by imagining it as a dance between *nourishment* and *pruning*. These words are not only common ways of considering the growth of plant life, but they also can be effectively applied to the processes by which neural networks become more resilient.[14] In this sense, character benefits from nourishment that provides something for us that we otherwise do not have, while pruning restrains or takes away from our mind its activities that would otherwise lead to its disintegration.

NOURISHMENT

Of all the nourishment that a child needs, none is more significant than her secure attachment to her parents. All else flows from this. For human beings, we primarily find nourishment for the formation of character in the attachment relationship that the newborn and infant forms with her caregivers.[15] This then extends to our adult attachment relationships as we grow and develop.[16] All remaining nourishing efforts, even those to meet her physical/material requirements, are an outgrowth of the dance between our longing as the caretakers of the child for the child to be loved and the child's looking for someone looking for her. Hence, character development draws its nourishment from the soil of secure attachment.

In the same way, we Christians believe that all that is good is grounded in God's love for us. But as we have seen in earlier chapters, our actual perception of being loved involves the attachment mechanism created by God. To be loved by him, to be nourished by him, necessitates the activation of our attachment system.[17]

Attachment processes present the most effective way for us to regulate our emotional states. That is, in terms of developing healthy minds that love God with all that they are, coregulation is always preferable to our brains being left on their own to navigate a distressing emotional event.[18] The more insecurely attached we are to those in our lives with whom we share close emotional connections, the more likely we will attempt to self-regulate in isolation.

Over the course of Evelyn's time in treatment, culminating in her joining a confessional community, we focused on her becoming more aware of what her typical attachment pattern tended to be. It was a fusion of an anxious and avoidant form,[19] and as she became aware of this, she learned to pause and make better sense of what she was sensing even when what she was sensing was uncomfortable.

One way to express how this process of attachment unfolds is the degree to which the child experiences being seen, soothed, safe, and secure, the 4 S's explored earlier.[20] We use the sturdy base of being seen, soothed, and safe to move out into the world of security—a place in which we take proper risks, make non-catastrophic mistakes, get our feelings hurt, and endure ruptures that we learn to repair. In this, we face some of the most rugged moments of life, moments that can reveal our weaknesses and the places where we respond to them by relying on our addictions and idols.

But they are also the moments in which we participate in the creation of the most durable beauty and goodness, and so bear and reflect the trinitarian God in whose image we have been made. Made to create in the way that he creates. Within the confessional community, these moments of risk also provide the opportunity for the most breathtaking generativity, which you have seen for Evelyn, Wendy, and many of the others you have met thus far.

But not every aspect of our stories advances to a place of security at the same rate. Neurally, networks correlated with our unhealed, unresolved traumas continue to be activated by events even as our healing process proceeds, as we witnessed with Wendy in the last chapter. Hence, we need to return to be "with" those networks so as to slowly "convert" them and bathe them in the neuroelectrical activity of empathic connection with the minds of others, the neural activation of being seen, soothed, and safe. These unhealed parts of our stories can quickly and unexpectedly be exposed as our implicit memories of old wounds are activated. Thus, in literally microseconds, we can find ourselves transported to states of mind in which we feel much more like children again, rather than the adult selves we are.

On one occasion, at the commencement of one of our group sessions, another woman commented to Evelyn how much she liked the dress Evelyn was wearing. Without warning, Evelyn suddenly felt herself awash with fear, her face turning red and her hands shaking. She reported a tightening in her throat and a shortening of her breath. Tears began to form.

The woman who had spoken to her was taken aback but quickly asked what was happening for Evelyn. It turned out that Evelyn had conversed with her older sister the day before, the sister who had for so many years mistreated her, the one who had taken her clothes. The conversation ended abruptly, as was so often the case, when her sister hung up on Evelyn since she would not agree to her sister's terms regarding a possible upcoming visit.

Evelyn was not aware of how much that conversation with her sister had primed her to have an adverse response when her confessional community comember commented on the attractiveness of her dress. That comment, intended to be an act of kindness and love, landed within Evelyn's state of mind not merely as a woman's thoughtful affirmation of her dress but rather as tantamount to a warning of its impending theft— and prompted the anticipation that no one would come to her aid in the process. This reactivated the embodied neural networks correlated with the memories of those traumas—hence Evelyn's negative response to this well-intended gesture of goodwill and connection.

As unpleasant as this experience was for Evelyn, it gave us the chance to once again nourish Evelyn's being—to enable her to be seen and soothed and to rest in knowing that she was safe. This took the better part of ten minutes and included participation from several members of the group.

This opportunity helped Evelyn to develop even greater security in her attachment to each of us—and to Jesus, whom she is continually more able to imagine as being in the room with her. Moreover, as she engages in more of these kinds of moments over time, she develops greater capacity to notice what she is feeling, to draw on the presence of the community, and to bring herself more quickly and seamlessly to a place of comfort and confidence. This is character being formed in real time. *But there was more.*

As Evelyn persevered over weeks and months through the repeated cycles of her story in this way, increasing her resilience in the face of different memories, her comfort and confidence enabled her to see her story with greater objectivity.[21] In so doing, she reported, "I feel older, like my real age, like an adult. I don't feel like that twelve-year-old little girl. I even am aware of feeling sorry for my sister when before all I felt was fear and rage. I am calm in my body, and I am thinking so differently. There was a time I would never have imagined I could feel this way."

Her character traits of peace, patience, kindness, and goodness were deepening, and she could sense them doing so in her very body. She was becoming more merciful, and she felt that mercy's durability. And all as a direct result of her persevering work in the face of her suffering in the presence of a vulnerable community.

Like Evelyn, I, too, have had my own moments of revisiting implicitly recalled memories that I don't like, times when I could use some help being seen, soothed, safe, and secure.

Not long ago, when having a conversation with my wife about finances, I said to her that when we talk about this issue in particular, I sometimes feel like I'm about ten years old. I feel uninformed, even stupid.

Not that I'm not smart enough to know how money works. I am and I do, and I'm not as uninformed overall as I feel in that moment. I know how to balance a budget and not overspend. I know that saving money is important, that tithing is the bedrock of how we even begin to imagine what money is—that it is a gift from God that I want to steward well. But actually having to consider developing a vision for finance still leaves me feeling much, much younger than I am.

Money, despite being something my parents talked with me about when I was young, was not a topic we regularly visited. This and many other significant matters of life were not discussed—what it means to be a follower of Jesus, beyond that it is the right thing to do; relationships in general, women and sex in particular; what it means to be a male; the nature and purpose of education, and why to attend college and which one; and what work is for, beyond paying the bills.

My parents were not equipped to even be aware that such conversations should take place, let alone to initiate them with me. This didn't make them bad people or parents; I am quite proud to have had them as my father and mother. Moreover, that they were ill-equipped is not something I hold against them. Nonetheless, I was left to figure these things out on my own, and I was not a gold mine of wisdom at age ten—the age I occasionally find myself feeling developmentally when speaking with my wife about money.

Accordingly, in these conversations I sometimes respond

anxiously or, more commonly, avoidantly, assuming (as I know to be the case) that my wife has a handle on these things. This of course gives me great comfort—but only reinforces my tendency to remain my ten-year-old self, which is not very attractive to her. You get the picture.

Despite the challenge that I present to my wife on these occasions, even then she works hard to provide the opportunity for me to feel seen, soothed, safe, and secure. But as anyone reading this who is married knows, married couples are not perfect at this for each other. In fact, we need outside resources that fortify each member of the couple to be for each other what they most long to be, with each being formed more fully into the image of Jesus.

During those conversations with my wife, I realize that although just the two of us are talking, my parents—in all their silence—are in the room and in on the conversation, leaving me to make my way on my own as to what to do about our IRA. It's not easy in those moments for my wife to be married to a ten-year-old, nor does she want to be. It is because of moments like these that I need my own cloud of witnesses—as does she—my own company of sentinels who I can imagine being in the room with me. Moreover, I also need to do the work of paying regular visits—not just a onetime thing—to my ten-year-old self to offer him the chance to be seen, soothed, safe, and secure. Nourishment of this kind enables me, enables any of us, to embody that "[we have] died, and [our] life is now hidden with Christ in God."[22]

Intuitively, the concept of nourishment would typically engender notions of receiving what we need from someone else who can provide it; we are the needy one looking for help. But, somewhat counterintuitively, nourishment is also something we can receive by giving ourselves away. As Karl Menninger has reminded us, giving ourselves away in service to another is one of the primary ways we can begin to move out of a state of depression.[23] In this way, giving ourselves to others does not merely "help" them nor merely help us feel better about ourselves because we *have* helped them; rather, to serve others in any way requires that we become vulnerable, even if we are the ones on the higher level of the power gradient. We put ourselves in the position of being hurt, rejected, or exposed anytime we do this. It is in giving to others explicitly out of our vulnerability that we are deeply nourished.

This requires risk, and none other than Jesus himself provides our model. In John's Gospel, Jesus meets a Samaritan woman at a well and asks her for a drink of water.[24] From where I sit, I am tempted to assume that the only way to read this story is as one in which Jesus is in complete control of the entire narrative from start to finish; there is no contingency here.

We imagine that his being thirsty, albeit true to his physical condition at the time, is actually only a setup for the *real* conversation, a ploy to draw the woman in, as if his thirst isn't really all that important other than to provide him with a provocative metaphor for where he is really going. He's not really *that* thirsty. I mean, he's the Son of Man. This only highlights how easy it is for me to limit the depth of the mystery of Jesus's humanity—just as it is easy for me to limit the depth of my own humanity or that of others around me.

But what if the woman had flat-out refused to give him a drink or, for that matter, refused to continue the conversation with him? What then of his thirst? Would he simply call an audible and move to a different metaphor in order to get her attention? Perhaps.

But I want to pay attention to the possibility that *it was Jesus's genuine need—his vulnerability*—that sets the stage for what comes next. It appears that his willingness as a Jewish male to become vulnerable took the woman by surprise. Yes, there is the obvious move *not* to use his position of power; but he takes it even further by asking for help.

It would not have surprised me had the woman been completely unwilling to move forward in the conversation, given her experience with men. I am not making theological claims that the text does not demonstrate. I am, rather, noting that Jesus's genuine vulnerability appears to be one of the most significant interpersonal dynamics moving the dialogue along. What stands out even more is what happens when his disciples return from the town, having gone to find food.

They are flummoxed that he has somehow been nourished while they were gone—but with what? He answers them straightforwardly. "'My food,' said Jesus, 'is to do the will of him who sent me and to finish his work.'"[25] His having done the work his Father had given him to do *with the Father and in the Father's presence* was his nourishment. This included *finishing* the work. And Jesus's comment here points forward to what finishing the work really meant—crucifixion.[26]

As I consider which part of doing "the will of him who sent me" was so nourishing, my imagination is easily limited in its scope. That his conversation with the woman led to a favorable outcome for her and her community seems the obvious answer to the disciples' question. But it still required Jesus to be vulnerable with no guarantee of what the outcome would be.

Moreover, John has Jesus including *the finishing* as the ultimate act of vulnerability in which there was no good in sight for the disciples on the Friday we now call Good. On that day, hope was not to be found. On that day, vulnerability seemed to be on the wrong side of history.

For Jesus, nourishment certainly included the sense of pleasure at the newly redeemed life that was emerging in that Samaritan woman and then in the entire town. But it first required his being vulnerable, foreshadowing that which would be required of him at the end, at his crucifixion. Here Jesus demonstrates that in vulnerably giving of ourselves, we create the possibility for others to be nourished—which in turn circles back around to joyfully nurture us as well, in this case Jesus's joy at being loved by the woman in response to her being loved by him.

In this same way, just as Evelyn had come to know the nourishment that came from being receptive to love from the others in her community, it first required her to be vulnerable, and repeatedly so. And from her vulnerability, from the love she received in others' empathy, she also witnessed how her vulnerability enabled *them* to take similar risks.

The risk Jesus took with the Samaritan woman led to her willingness to trust him, which was an actual gift of nourishment to him. He was not someone who needed nothing from this relationship; he longed to be connected to her in the same way that he knew of her need of connection to him. Her response, her turning in love toward him, was part of the nourishment, part of the matrix of Jesus doing the will of his Father.

This practice of vulnerably giving ourselves away—including, repeatedly, those parts of us that are weak or unattractive—has the effect of infusing others with the inspiration and courage needed to do likewise and so find the same freedom that Evelyn was discovering. Evelyn's vulnerability (which led to her receptivity to the love—the nourishment—of others) enabled others, in turn, to receive love more ably from her and each other as well in places where they too held their unfinished business of trauma.

The risk of being vulnerable became part of the source of her nourishment, the nourishment that is received through perseverance and is fundamental to the formation of character. Here we see how Evelyn's work encourages the work of her comembers, and in this way the body of Christ "builds itself up in love, as each part does its work."

PRUNING

In many respects, when we consider nourishment, as that of a tree, we are hinting at what we are *giving* to the tree, what the tree receives so as to flourish more fully. It is a way we say yes to the tree, and in our forming character, we are saying yes to what we need that sustains us.

Pruning consists of the actions that take something away from us—or maybe that we resist receiving—as part of the mission of character formation. In this sense, we are saying no to something we want that we don't have, or no to something we want to rid ourselves of.

We understand pruning as one of God's ways of loving us, most vividly communicated in Jesus's words to his disciples on the night he was betrayed.[27] He notes that he is the vine, we are branches, and his Father is the vine dresser. His Father prunes those branches that are bearing fruit such that they may bear even more. It is the case that God's "no" is as much a part of his love for us as is his "yes." It is, to be sure, challenging for us to delay gratification, to say no.[28]

Character formation requires that we say no to a great many things. No to distraction. No to overindulgence. No to devouring rather than desiring beauty, not least when it comes in the form of sex. No to consumption. No to violence.

Jesus knows all about "no." He said no in his temptations in the wilderness and then continued to say no on multiple occasions throughout his ministry, right to the very end.[29] I have every reason to believe that saying no was no easier for Jesus than it is for me.

But he said no to so much in order to say yes to so much more, and he bids us do the same. Yes to being receptive to love. Yes to repairing ruptures. Yes to revealing our brokenness in trustworthy, vulnerable community. Yes to showing generous hospitality. Yes to developing durable resilience. Yes to creating beauty and goodness.

But often, the no must precede the yes. Hence the writer of the letter to the Hebrews suggests that in order to run our race with perseverance, we must "throw off everything that hinders and the sin that so easily entangles."[30] Which, in simple interpersonal neurobiological terms, amounts to delaying gratification.

When we enter our favorite fast-food restaurant, especially one that others enjoy equally well, we often find a line of customers ahead of us. If the line is unusually short, we are pleased. If it is unusually long, we are not so pleased because we will have to wait—longer than we have anticipated—and thus we will have to delay gratification.

But if the line is what we expect it to be (I realize this is starting to sound like "Goldilocks and the Three Bears"), despite having to wait, our waiting is *within the time we have anticipated*. Hence, the waiting, the delay, is not just about the waiting in and of itself; it is matched against *what we had anticipated*. And what we anticipate is not an emotionless "fact of the future of which I happen to be aware." Our anticipation is tied up with our longings.

This correlation may seem patently obvious. But for Evelyn, learning to be patient had practical implications when it came to her perseverance and the formation of her character. At the very same time she was saying yes to being receptive to others' empathy, she was having to say no to the story in her mind in which she still longed for her parents' and siblings' attunement and love. She continued to imagine that they would, perhaps eventually, come through for her, despite all evidence to the contrary. She was having to give up a story—an idol, an addiction, if you will—which was painful for her to do. Who wants to be pruned of the reasonable desire for your parents to love you? It would feel like cutting off your right arm.

But when that desire only ever leads to disappointment and sadness, giving it up may be the only thing one can resort to. This process itself (that no one ever enjoys) can lead initially to its own form of distress and irritability—its own form of suffering. Just like the way I can become irritable when I am suddenly faced with the feeling of disappointment when I don't get something I really wanted. Like chocolate chip cookies.

My wife makes the best chocolate chip cookies. In. The. World. Whenever she does, and whatever the occasion, without fail, I am suddenly a two-year-old scouting to ensure that there will be enough—for me. My heart rate picks up the moment I sense she is being a bit too generous with how many she intends for others to have, thus how many I will *not* have.

And so I take them. Three or four at a time. Mind you, not in some obvious way and not in broad daylight. I even ask permission if I can have one or two, looking to take four or five. You would think it was my last meal. And of course, if it were, my wife's cookies would be fitting for the menu. But it's not my last meal. They're cookies.

It's funny, cookies. How on earth do they so easily reveal the flimsiness of my character? As we know, at the end of the day, it's not about cookies. It's about the part of me that feels so alone with emptiness that it moves to hoard and clutch even the most relatively insignificant thing as a way to keep the sadness that dwells underneath the emptiness at bay.

And so, as odd as it sounds, my relationship with chocolate chip cookies is a dynamic that presents the opportunity for me to delay gratification, to say no to them (or at least six to eight at a time) so that I can say yes to Jesus—and others, my wife not the least. First, I invite that part of me that is filled with sadness into the room where Jesus is, and then I allow him to be genuinely comforted by Jesus, by me, and by others so as to enable him to grow, hopefully from a two-year-old to someone older, perhaps even eventually to adulthood.

But this growth in character requires pruning. Not just of cookies but of my fierce protection of that part of me that carries the sadness so as to allow it to be seen, soothed, safe, and eventually secure. In allowing this pruning to take place, I become someone who can take enormous delight in chocolate chip cookies in moderation because I know in my very body that even one or two of them are coming right from the hands of Jesus who is winking at me with kindness and confidence as he offers them to me.

Another aspect of pruning and of learning to delay gratification comes in the form of how we engage relational ruptures. These amount to any form of relational disruption, be it minor or severe, whose hallmark is a sense of disconnection associated with emotional distress. IPNB provides categories of *oscillating/benign*, *limit-setting*, and *toxic* ruptures (which is notable for the degree to which shame is mobilized as a key element of the rupture).[31]

It has been postulated that our attachment process is mediated through the social engagement system, explored earlier in chapter 1. In essence, we navigate the world and regulate our emotional states most effectively through this system, and strengthening it is one of the ways the character we long for is formed.[32] Like all living systems, our minds flourish and become more resilient only by facing a proper amount of stress over time. This happens in many ways, one of which includes our encounters with ruptures. Ed Tronick's work in attachment reveals how vital to growth is the repair of ruptures; when repairs don't take place, growth is hampered.[33]

But I don't know anyone who actually *enjoys* the prospect of repairing ruptures. At least, not like I enjoy chocolate chip cookies. To initiate the repair of a ruptured relationship or even to accept another's invitation to repair a rupture they have perpetrated with you often requires a great deal of courage—and the delay of gratification, the short-term gratification that I experience by avoiding the work involved in repairing the rupture.

On one occasion, as I expressed my felt sense of protection for Evelyn as she spoke of her sister's behavior, she quickly began to withdraw emotionally. My colleague Courtney, attuned to what she saw happening, drew Evelyn's attention to her and began, in very slow and deliberate fashion, to help Evelyn describe what had just happened between the two of us. She was able to help Evelyn express that what she sensed coming from me reminded her of the fear she felt when her older siblings would ridicule or dismiss her. Gradually my colleague was able to persuade Evelyn to turn her gaze, literally, back in my direction. (She had, for the entire time she was speaking with Courtney, looked only at her and not at me—she couldn't, as it was too unsettling.)

We then were able to initiate the process of repair with me first assuring Evelyn that I cared for her well-being. Next, I acknowledged that what I had said and how I had said it had frightened her and even hurt her; that I in no way wanted to do that; that it grieved me that I had done so; that I longed for her forgiveness; and that I would work to be careful not to repeat that blunder in the future. I did *not* say that what I had said was "wrong"; I was emphasizing my sadness that I had hurt her and my intention to be more mindful in the future about how

I spoke with her. Over the next several minutes, we worked in our dance of repair to not only bring our relationship back to where it had been but propel it forward to an even more resilient place than it had been before the rupture occurred.

This does not explain the total picture of our interaction, but it gets at the heart of how repairing ruptures is a form of pruning that cannot be emphasized enough, one that we quite seamlessly go to great lengths to avoid. In this pruning, we say no to our automatic tendency to protect ourselves by avoiding the repair so that we can say yes to deeper relationships—especially those in which we have been hurt by or have hurt others. Those who in those moments have become our enemies. Our enemies for whom Jesus has commanded we pray and toward whom we desire to commit acts of lovingkindness.

This is not to be understood as trusting others who are untrustworthy—that is a different conversation. Here I am simply offering the repair of ruptured relationships as yet another way that pruning leads to the durable formation of character, a practice in which we persevere in the context of vulnerable community.

And with the perseverance of nourishment and pruning, character is not only what we become; it is the very feature out of which the hope that does not put us to shame is born.

Born to live. Born to thrive. Born to remind us of the glory of God that the Holy Trinity longs for us to share.

Chapter Eight

HOPE

◆

...and character, hope...

ROMANS 5:4B

As we move from character to hope, we soon discover that hope is not something we merely "hope" emerges. We will become increasingly hopeful *not* as a function of simply attempting to "be hopeful," as if we could conjure it on demand. It will not develop as a result of me gathering up my courage and making myself "believe" or "feel" something that seems close to what I imagine hope to be. Rather, it will develop indirectly, as a byproduct of the persevering work we do in response to suffering.

The word *hope* points to our future—we hope for what is coming, for the future we anticipate. That anticipated future, that hope, is based, however, on what we remember from our past. We are only able to anticipate things when we already have some idea of them based on a memory of a past experience. For that past to provide the resources for a *hopeful* future, it must consist of events that have themselves been experienced positively in some way.

These positive experiences are not limited to ones of immediate well-being; they can also include ones in which we have endured and persevered in the face of suffering. Hope is formed in durable ways especially when that suffering is enveloped in a deeply sensed, felt, imaged, and thoughtfully considered awareness of being loved. Outpouring, self-giving love that is the glory of God we come to know most intimately, most powerfully, in the context of the vulnerable body of Jesus.

This is not to suggest that we *only* arrive at hope through suffering. So much of what we imagine our hopeful future to be is grounded in our remembered past. And in hope's case, those recollections of joyful experiences of beauty and goodness will fuel our anticipation of that very future.

We marry someone because the relationship we have shared thus far is one of lovingkindness by which we have generated a growing sense of life together, one of an expanding, similar nature. We hope that our favorite team plays well because we have had *enough* experience of joy and celebration in the past to warrant our willingness to imagine that *this* might be the season. We are hopeful for this summer's vacation plans because the notion of traveling to Yosemite National Park is one of great beauty and because we have successfully planned and had lovely vacations in the past.

We hope that our child can be cured of his cancer because there is the memory of our deep love for him and because there is *enough* evidence in the past that some people's cancer can be healed. People come to our practice because they have enough evidence from enough people that the work of psychotherapy has been helpful.

In all these examples, hope is so patently self-evident that we barely even consider it being in play. Nevertheless, it is still a function of the temporal domain of integration, that feature of our mind by which we generate and then perceive a thing called a "future," one based on our similarly generated and perceived (remembered) "past."[1] It is obviously far easier to be hopeful in response to life events that are more immediately gratifying—events that we more frequently and naturally assume to be a source of hope.

We do not automatically assume hope to emerge from painful, difficult circumstances. And although the generation of hope requires our remembered past from which it will spring, our past or present circumstances can't guarantee a hopeful future. Things can be fine one second and then suddenly not. Just ask Job. And, as it turns out, the challenges of suffering create the opportunities for us to form the hope that is most durable.

The enterprise of developing durable hope is far from easy. First, the forces of evil actively resist our work to form hope, enmeshed as they are in the painful experiences of daily life, not to mention those spiritual beings behind so much evil we encounter. Second, our memories of trauma and shame are so thoroughly neurally embedded that even when we have begun the journey of healing our traumatized pasts, we find that we must continue to work through those stories over and over again as we push against the ancient networks that have been wired to fire together so easily. All of this is then writ large in our experiences of the world around us.

When we search for hope, it is not always easy to access. The fact that then-Senator Barack Obama's 2004 Democratic National Convention speech drew such acclaim was due in no small part to hope being described as audacious.[2]

But this is not new, and we are not the first to hunger and thirst for hope as we do. The ancient Romans knew a thing or two about marketing it to a population who also longed for hope. In their case, hope for peace. Hence, *Pax Romana*. No matter that the founding of the nearly two-hundred-yearlong period of relative peace within the Roman Empire's borders came from the spear points of Roman legions, a peace maintained by the assurance that those same legions would be at your doorstep should you waver in your commitment to it.[3] This was not the peace of Jesus. Nevertheless, it reveals how hope was as important in the first century as it is now.

Little wonder, then, that the Bible is so replete with references to hope,[4] indicating how desperately we have needed it throughout history. Doubtless, people of each era could find reasons to believe that their circumstances were the most desperate ever known. In our own time, of course, we have our particular take on that universal longing.

At the time of the Plague of Justinian (541–544 CE), no one could anticipate that medical science would identify *Yersinia pestis* and develop an effective treatment, eliminating the disease. They may have been shocked and terrified that a third of Constantinople's population was being wiped out. They weren't surprised or indignant that their doctors hadn't prevented it in the first place; rather, they more easily blamed the gods, or God, who was obviously angry with Justinian.[5] But there was no sense that humankind, with all the power of its medical technology, should have been able to prevent it. Science, as we know it, didn't exist. Unlike in our era, people did not look to science to solve their problems.

The last five hundred years, however, have given us reason to assume scientific discovery plausible within the cultural latticework of the Enlightenment and modernity that has supported it. These developments have rested heavily on our love affair with the human mind's capacity for rational thought and the associated presumption that somehow we are more capable than were Adam and Eve of carrying the weight of becoming gods by knowing the difference between good and evil.

This era of discovery has also inculcated within us the tacit sense of not only what we can and do know but just as importantly *how* we come to know anything at all.[6] Nevertheless, scientific advances have made our lives truly, in general, more comfortable and convenient—which is no small thing. For example, relatively speaking, poverty is less prevalent than it was even one hundred years ago.[7] Not only *that* a vaccine was developed for the COVID-19 virus but that it was developed as quickly as it was remains nothing short of remarkable.

However, such advances have subtly and steadily lulled us into a state of presuming that we, especially in the more affluent West, are impregnable to disaster. Not that we think this consciously. No one would admit that nothing catastrophic could happen to us. We're too smart for that. But that's not how we *live*. That the development of our sense of invulnerability has taken place over such a long time is part of what has strengthened and maintained it. We have been practicing under the banner of what we call "progress" for far longer than we know, passing neurally correlated assumptions along from generation to generation.

Such assumptions amount to, "We, on our own as humans, can and will figure it out. Whatever *it* may be." As such, with the appearance of something like COVID-19 and its prolonged assault on, yes, our bodies, but more significantly on our belief in our cultural invulnerability, our longing for hope is that much more desperate. Not that we were consciously aware of this assumption; rather, the pandemic exposed it. Exposed *us*. The virus did not *cause* our fragility so much as *revealed* it.

In contrast to the ancient Hebrew and Christian tradition that tells the story of humans as continually and inescapably repeating our parents' and their parents' disintegration, brokenness, and violence (our sin), the extended period of material progress has inculcated an alternate assumption— that the basic human condition and its moral expression are somehow improving along with our technological advances, a course of progression that the founders of the Enlightenment naively expected. We of modernity believe and are taught that, everything being equal, we are more well behaved than our ancestors.[8]

But when we look closely at how we continue to act, not least in developed countries, nothing indicates that we are, at our core, better human beings now than we have been. We are a frightened people. We are a shame-sodden people. We are a violent people committed to promoting a culture of death, most often able to make peace only by threatening more war.

We are a people who consume our relationships and the earth in the process. We commit acts of injustice and then respond to those injustices by offering our own versions of justice, versions that come with enough meanness to choke a horse.[9] Over the course of the last many months, the COVID-19 pandemic revealed how increasingly isolated and fragile we are.

We have never been more affluent—yet, simultaneously, never more anxious or depressed.[10] We are more easily offended and more frequently declare how "unsafe" we are. So unsafe, in fact, that the very word "safe" has virtually lost its meaning due to the frequency of its misappropriation.[11]

In addition, as mentioned before, we become what we pay attention to, and we pay a great deal of attention to media, particularly social media. The most captivating content that we post and consume is also the most jarring and anxiety-provoking, despite those very posts being offered by a relatively small number of account holders.[12] This dynamic creates in the imaginations of many the conviction that the number of people who think and behave radically differently than they do is far greater than it is in reality.[13]

In response to this, to calm our mostly self-generated anxiety, we desperately, urgently look for those who think like we think about any number of things, while simultaneously we dismiss or demonize anyone who thinks differently than we do. Counterintuitively, this act, while temporarily assuaging our fear as we find and place ourselves in the company of those who are most like us, has the longer-term effect of reinforcing and strengthening our fear of the other side, which leads to further demonization and fracture.

The front page of the *Washington Post* recently carried the story of a meeting at the White House between the president and a group of academic historians who are quite worried that democracy is teetering on the edge of collapse and who hoped to bring to his attention what dire straits we are in.[14] Neither the historians nor the *Post* seemed very hopeful.

We have placed a great deal of our emotional security, even our very souls' security, in liberal democracy and its associated counterpart of capitalism. Both of these philosophies are, in their—in our—better moments, worthy of measured, limited trust as well-intended institutions.

Our difficulty lies in our failure to regularly consider that it is *we*, human beings, who both construct and place our hope in them. We who have yet to plumb the depths of our traumas, wounds, brokenness, grief, and sin, as Flannery O'Connor would suggest[15]—and therefore our capacity to commit violence. Rather, we continue to act them out despite and in the face of all our progress. Many metrics of social anxiety in the general population indicate that people are more anxious now than we were thirty years ago.[16] This is not just because the times are tough—and they are. It is in no small part because we expect they shouldn't be. We are not explicitly aware of this. Rather, we have tacitly been trained to assume this illusion as the way life should be over many, many years.

The people of the first century did not live with illusions such as these. Not, of course, that those to whom Paul was writing had no illusions or distractions at all. Theirs just took different forms and rested largely on the notion that they had little to no control over their fate (remember, the gods were at war with everyone; no one was safe). Whereas we have come to believe that, contrary to the evidence in front of us (it is still the case that no one gets out alive), we *can* control our fate.

Of course, if asked directly, we *know* rationally that we are not in charge of the universe; we just live as if we are. Hence, the agency of people of the first century was in the sacrifices they made to the gods and, when they were able, in being able to eat, drink, and be merry until they died.

We sacrifice to different gods. The gods of progress, which include our affluence and the convenience and comfort it affords, as well as the violence-enforced power to maintain it when and how necessary.

These preliminary reflections are merely intended to remind us that hope is not something that we construct in a vacuum. Rather, the degree to which we are hopeful depends on the attention we pay to forming it. And the degree to which our attention is taken up by something else—what the world offers—will result in a corresponding lack of hope.

At all times I, just like the ancients, am having to be vigilantly aware of the messages sent to me on behalf of the world, the flesh, and the devil that aspire to squeeze me into their mold.[17] Knowing about those principalities and powers external to me, along with the unresolved traumas and shame that I harbor in my neurally embedded body, is an essential awareness. For as it turns out, hope never exists on its own in the privacy of my mind. It is, as we will soon see, formed only in a community, with its mission being, surprisingly, that of locating something, or rather some*one*, in whom our future rests.

◆ ◆ ◆

Given that culture shapes the way we interact interpersonally and given the biblical writers' take on the gods[18]—in particular, Paul's assumptions about what he named as principalities and powers[19]—we most importantly must take stock of what we are up against when it comes to this activity of forming hope.

Indeed, one of the goals of evil is to keep us from becoming hopeful. For if we do, we are not just more likely to feel better about our lives but are more likely to actually love and pray for our enemies. We are likely to be less afraid to suffer in the service of Jesus and our neighbors, not least those with whom we have great difference. We do not live in a neutral universe, but evil is literally hell-bent on using our culture to persuade us that we do. Moreover, evil wants us to believe either that *it* doesn't exist or, if it does, that it only takes up residence in "someone else."

For our purposes, I am not imagining that hope "exists" fundamentally as an abstraction or an idea (notwithstanding those philosophers among you who will remind me of Plato's Ideal Forms). Rather, I am drawing your attention to hope as a particular state of mind. Of course, when Paul or anyone else uses the word, they are describing something they believe is real. But it is only real—and ultimately reliable—*as a function of a collaboratively creative interpersonal interaction in which our attention is directed to something other than ourselves that can faithfully fulfill our longings.*

We form hope not on our own but in the company of others; and we do so by collectively directing our attention to something outside of ourselves that we believe can provide the beauty and goodness we long for but cannot achieve on our own. It depends on something or someone else.

We hope that our vacation at Disney World is enjoyable. We hope the car is able to make it to the gas station before the tank runs dry. She hopes he likes her. He hopes she likes him. I hope the traffic clears out so I don't miss my flight. In all cases, our longing depends on something other than ourselves coming through for us but which we cannot control.

This is not rocket science; it's common sense. But despite its simplicity, it is still very hard, because we are talking about practicing trusting Jesus *now*. We practice trusting him directly and vicariously through our relationships with the members of his body; and we see the fruit of that trust as we have, over time, experienced being seen, soothed, safe, and secure (the 4 S's) and then have practiced remembering those moments.

But there is a great deal about the world and about my own remembered story that can keep me from trusting Jesus, keep me from practicing the 4 S's in such a way that I can experience the healing to be discovered in multiple present moments that collectively become the remembered past from which my hopeful, anticipated future emerges. This requires very, very hard work. And Shane came to know all about what hard work meant.

It began with a gambling addiction that led to embezzlement to fund the habit he could not control. Eighteen months in jail did not make things easier, although it did keep him from spending money he didn't have. The problem for Shane was not just his criminal record, which was bad enough. Worse was the brutality of his shame.

He graduated from college with a dual degree in finance and computer science. He was on the fast track for ascending the corporate ladder of a venture capital startup. He was smart and shrewd, which captured the attention of his C-suite bosses; those traits also helped him make quick money counting cards at the blackjack tables. As soon as he thought a casino was on to him, he moved on. He figured he could outsmart just about anyone. That is, until his ability to win at gambling began to fall short. In his anxious response, he threw good money after bad until he found a way to draw from the cash box of his firm. The movie didn't end well.

After prison, Shane had friends who invited him to live with them and arranged for him to begin working for a land-scape architect. His supervisor recognized his intelligence and savvy, especially as Shane made some humble yet confident remarks about ways for the company to extend its reach along with other suggestions for how to invest their profit back into the business in a way that would benefit everyone.

Outside of his job, Shane's social circle was limited to his ongoing effort in Gamblers Anonymous. For the first several months after his release from prison, most of his energy was directed to work and recovery. But as anyone might guess, one can grind away like that for only so long. Eventually, Shane began to feel more burdened by his shame and the way it made it difficult for him to venture out beyond the limits of the two groups of people he occupied. At the suggestion of the friend with whom he was living, he sought help in our practice. This led to the kind of journey embarked on by many who are look-ing for hope. From seeing me individually, he stepped into a confessional community where he opened to the members the recesses of his story that began long before his gambling habit.

Shane had grown up in a family that had sustained the generational trauma of his maternal grandmother having died unexpectedly from complications due to pregnancy when Shane's mother was four years old. Unsurprisingly, his mother eventually developed a great fear of being left, which manifested in numerous ways, not least being how tightly she clung to her own children. To escape the suffocation he felt from her, Shane had spent hours in his room playing video games and reading.

He was successful in school, but he had never been comfortable with peer relationships, in no small part because he had received limited modeling of how to confidently navigate them. Always he had felt a subtle but undeniable undercurrent of distress when faced with social circumstances that were novel or that included a large number of unfamiliar people.

For Shane, academics were a haven, his place of comfort. However, although being smart temporarily reduced his anxiety, it didn't increase his sense of confidence in the relational interactions where he needed it most. Then he found that counting cards gave him access to a bolus of dopamine that no perfect report card could. And it didn't require his having to build a relationship with a human being in order to acquire it.

It was no surprise, then, that he found himself in my office with a gambling addiction that was actually his way of compensating for his relational distress, distress that was due to his minimal experience of the 4 S's. When he first entered psychotherapy, he would have said that he was hoping to be rid of his addiction. But eventually, he discovered that durable hope is formed by directing your attention to creating something that does not yet exist.

What did not yet exist for Shane was enough practice genuinely trusting others with whom he could form hope in a durable fashion. Little by little, however, he began to enter into that practice. It began in his recovery meetings and continued with his sponsor. It deepened in his individual psychotherapy and accelerated in his work in a confessional community.

But it was not easy to do. On multiple occasions in the community, as Shane revealed yet one more event in which his mother had emotionally suffocated him, he would literally become short of breath while speaking. And no wonder, for his mother's behavior of this kind continues to this day. Every time they interact, his old neural networks are activated, and he finds himself wanting to flee not just her but any and all relationships and to run for the proverbial blackjack tables.

Early on in his journey in the community, with each instance of this painful replay of old childhood wounds, Shane would find himself only able to visualize being in the casino, hearing the noises, smelling the aromas. And this would be followed by a deep sense of despair. Despair that he was unable to stop his reaction. He was not able—as far as he could tell—to generate hope for his future.

However, with each small interaction with the community, describing yet another difficult interchange with his mother or expressing that he couldn't see ever returning to work in finance because of his felony record, he would experience his sadness and despair being held by the members of the group, each in their own particular way. They would respond with empathy—but also with confidence in Shane's ability to continue to walk on this path because they were not leaving the room. They were going to walk on it with him. They affirmed how difficult his road was and how proud of him they were that he was walking it. Each one continued to remain present *and hopeful* for him.

Initially, although Shane could acknowledge his experience

of feeling seen and felt in those brief moments, they were so novel that he didn't initially encode them permanently in his memory. There simply was not yet enough neural network density firing with that correlated recollection. Even as he was feeling the connection with one of the other members, his mind would fill with images of his mother and the next conversation with her he anticipated having, and he would begin to feel the pull once more into sadness, followed at once by his imagining the rush of relief from winning back his money.

This familiar cycle would only heighten his frustration with how hard this process was, along with feelings of discouragement and pessimism. Moreover, the very act of his moving in his mind toward places of vulnerability quite understandably evoked a simultaneous sensation of panic. He had little experience yet to trust how the community would respond to him.

Shane's story, and the stories of many of the rest of us and the work involved in telling them more truly, does not suggest that any and all forms of pain can be eliminated simply by the sufferer having one or two conversations with someone. Just ask the victim of cancer or the person who has sustained sexual abuse. Another's presence does not immediately eradicate one's pain in either of those settings, and neither did it do so for Shane. What was required was perseverance, which is required for all of us.

For indeed, with perseverance, with multiple encounters of being seen, soothed, safe, and secure, I become more connected to those around me who see me—and, by extension, to the God who sees me. As I have these experiences and pay attention to them, I encode them in memory. And from that memory of being comforted in my pain, in my suffering, emerges my anticipation of a future in which I am able to imagine comfort, comfort even of an eternal nature in the future that Scripture tells us is coming. The heaven that is coming to earth, at which point it will be delivered of all its groaning.

Thus, I hope, not because someone has told me a story of a future time in which the new heaven and earth will appear and I simply "believe" it. In the face of suffering, belief of that type is not enough to sustain hope. Instead, I hope because I have formed it by practicing being loved and loving others in ways that I can remember, remember in embodied form. Thereby, I imagine a future of which these memories are a foretaste.

Perseverance of this kind leads to my becoming more aware of my connection to God and others and less attached to my pain, as Shane and so many others have discovered. Those willing to enter into this hard work pick up their crosses, crosses that represent the suffering of swimming against the current of the old stories they have carried for most of their lives. Picking up my cross includes, often ironically, allowing myself to become increasingly receptive to love, which necessarily requires me to enter into those painful parts of my story to which I have not yet given myself access in the presence of Jesus and others.

Although the details of their stories were different, Paul would have known fundamentally what Shane was experiencing. The former persecutor of Jesus knew a thing or two about what it meant to carry shame for having violently abused people, all for the cause of God, no less. Hope for the disciples would have arisen through their embodied encounter with the risen Christ—and for Paul, hope necessarily would have been born out of the same encounter, that on the road to Damascus.

But more durably, over time Paul's hope would have been built up more by his encounters with Jesus's followers, the ones he would go on to describe with the word "body." Imagine, in light of how Paul had treated them, the impact it would have had upon him *not* to be treated in like kind by Jesus and his followers. In response to Paul's violence, they met him with kindness and forgiveness. He was stopped in his tracks by it, in fact. Just as Shane was also stopped. These encounters continued to make possible Shane's going in the direction of beauty and goodness.

Thus, gradually, with more and more practice—with perseverance—through many repeated moments of sensing himself being seen, soothed, safe, and secure, Shane collected a large enough critical mass of experiences with the group that he began to recall these positive experiences more easily. As the group continued to be present for him, over time as he would tell of yet another of his mother's exploits, he noted that he was less acutely activated by her behavior.

More and more often, anytime a negative encounter with his mother occurred, he would bring the group members to mind and see, hear, and even feel in his body their being with him, comforting him and granting him the confidence to be less anxious. He was becoming more hopeful. And he was doing so because he and the group were forming hope within him and between each other.

As the community journeyed with Shane over many months, I often reminded them that they were being the body of Jesus for Shane and for each other; theirs was the embodied work of the Holy Spirit. We explored how the hope that Shane was forming—and that the others in the community were forming as well, as a result of his willingness to trust them, to form earned secure attachment with them—was not so much a "thing" that he "had" as an individual or that the community had as a whole. It was *a way in which Shane had grown to direct his attention* toward each of the other members of the community, anticipating that each one would be present and respond with lovingkindness no matter what Shane brought into the room. He was, in fact, "hoping" as it were *in a person*, in a collective body of persons. And the Person behind all of this was Jesus. Jesus, as embodied by the others in the room. Jesus, not in some metaphoric manner to which we often limit him but in the very form in which he promised he would be with us: in his body and in the Spirit.

To this form of the presence of Jesus our imaginations must extend. We must persevere in bringing our suffering into his presence by doing so in the presence of others. For hope to be real, we must direct our attention to something or someone else outside of ourselves who has the agency to change our experience of ourselves.

Yes, in one way, Shane "had" hope. But in another, he did not "have" it so much as he *anticipated a hopeful future* because of his repeated experiences of the present moment with other people who represented Jesus.

Here we must remember that hope was not something Shane developed on his own in isolation. For indeed, it is always co-constructed, which inevitably raises the question, "With whom am I cocreating the hope that I long for?"

As the community did this together and as Shane reported about interactions with his mother and other areas where he was increasing in comfort and confidence, he also noted that he was more able to imagine alternative futures for himself that included a return in some way to the world of finance. In essence, due to his mind's work in developing a greater payload of neural real estate that represented earned secure attachment, he paid less and less attention both implicitly and explicitly to his shame and the hold it had even in his body.

He eventually was able to initiate a conversation with the owner of the landscaping company for which he worked. Together they arranged for Shane to begin to advise the rest of the employees about their finances and how to plan for investments of even small amounts of money.

Word eventually got around that Shane was helping people in this way. Then came the moment when Shane opened his own financial planning firm. And when he did, he was amazed at where he found himself. But no one in the confessional community was amazed. For indeed, they had witnessed a man who had come into their presence in the fullness of suffering yet willing to reveal his story vulnerably, repeatedly, perseveringly, with all of its longings, griefs, traumas, and shame. And as a function of his perseverance, they had also witnessed the development of durable character; character from which hope emerged as a predictable byproduct.

And this hope in a future that was centered around the agency of Jesus became that which not only did not put him to shame but provided for Shane the reminder of a past that was continually being transformed, renewed as a firstfruits of the kingdom of God, fruit that heralds God's kingdom that is coming in its fullness.

But we also must remember that we do not live in a neutral universe, and evil is not about to go quietly into the night.

It is easy for me to want to believe that once I have begun to establish hope as a function of my suffering, at some point the suffering will either dissolve completely or do so enough that it won't bother me. Remember—I want to read a book about suffering and hope that will make suffering a thing of the past for me. But that is not the world in which we live.

It is fair to say that the more we suffer in the way of the cross, that is, in the way of Jesus, in the way of persevering toward the light in vulnerable community that is committed to the person of Jesus, the deeper our character will be and the more like Jesus we will become. Consequently, the more robust and durable our hope will be. But not because we simply try harder to hope. Rather, it is because we continue to submit ourselves to the presence of Jesus, who is with us in love in the face of our suffering.

Only Jesus can transform suffering into hope in the way that he does through the activity and power of the Holy Spirit and through his body of followers. *This* is why the news about suffering and the hope that we are to discover in it is better than we imagine. It is to this news so full of comfort and confidence—so full of hope—that we now turn, news that brings us full circle in our exploration of this portion of Paul's letter, that forms us into a people of hope and healing.

Chapter Nine

FULL CIRCLE

◆

And hope does not put us to shame, because God's
love has been poured out into our hearts through
the Holy Spirit, who has been given to us.

ROMANS 5:5

All the people whom you have met in this book at some point found themselves in a place of deep suffering. Whether they came to it as a result of what had happened to them, what they had done to themselves, or a combination thereof, they made the decision to begin the difficult, glorious journey toward wholeness, toward the holy, Trinitarian God.

In order to address their suffering, each person had to confront the reality and depth of the insecure nature of their attachment to God and to others as the result of their trauma and shame. Gradually they worked to receive the peace that was offered to each and every part of themselves that still believed it was at war with God.

In doing so, they became increasingly comfortable and confident working through their trauma, fear, and shame one small step at a time. Persevering in this way, they created new neural networks that became highly correlated and increasingly durable, networks that they could access and activate with greater consistency anytime they encountered situations that reignited the traumatic elements of their stories.

In the rewiring of their brains, they have developed character leading to the formation of hope by embedding more and more continually in their memories their experiences of being seen, soothed, safe, and secure—actively, consciously, intentionally, and *communally*. Such hope is the future one naturally anticipates as a consequence of all the work that has preceded it. Work that is frequently *born and conducted in the crucible of suffering*.

Suffering begins with pain—but becomes *suffering* because of our isolation and powerlessness in its presence. Only by risking being receptive to love—something that is very hard for us to do—will we form durable hope. This love is found initially in God coming to find us in Jesus, a journey that began with his pursuit of Adam and Eve. Thus, we see that hope is something we form in response to the loving presence of someone else. It is not something we manufacture on our own.

This durable hope that we co-form in the power and presence of the Holy Spirit and in the context of vulnerable community—this anticipated future in which someone is continually with us, coming to find us, and promising to come again (in the second coming of Jesus) *does not put us to shame.*

Other English translators have Paul saying that this hope "does not disappoint," which is saying the same thing, as we understand the fundamental emotional feature of disappointment is shame. I am disappointed, ultimately, in my circumstances because *I am not enough* to change them. We do not just take this in as a fact (I could not stop the hurricane that ruined our vacation to Disney World); we *feel deeply* the sense of loss of whatever it is *that we cannot prevent.*

But when we look closely, Paul emphasizes that this hope that we have formed is *not*, in and of itself, the reason we are not put to shame. Rather, the hope that we have co-labored to construct bears witness to the *person who loves us and has been given to us to help us form it*. It is not a *what*, but a *Who* that has been given to us. A person who has been coming to find us from the beginning, whose presence in Jesus is the fullness of Trinitarian expression, whose Spirit has been given to dwell within and between us as evidence of his faithful commitment to love us by being with us, guiding us to where he wants us to go.

You saw it, right? The Spirit is *given*. It was so unlike the gods to give anyone anything without strings attached. Who gives you anything but that you don't wonder to some degree about the strings? These would have been mind-bending words from the apostle. The Spirit is not someone we must acquire by working hard enough to overcome our shame and thereby prove our worthiness of receiving him.

But as we have seen, becoming receptive to love can prove to require harder work than we might assume. This is because love is not abstract; it is fully embodied, both in Jesus and in his members, whose eye contact, tone of voice, and body language—along with their words—are present for us in the material world.

This love does not exist in its fullness just in our imaginations, where we can make it out to be what we want, for good or for bad. No, it is right there in the room, providing the opportunity for the healing of your traumas while changing the neural networks of your brain in the process. This embodied love, when we receive it and are transformed by it in the very presence of our suffering, returns us over and over again to an ever stronger, more trusting relationship with Jesus and his body—this grace—in which we now stand.

We in fact "stand" in this grace because it is embodied in real time and space. And as we do so, our perception of our suffering itself is transformed through repeated experiences of the embodied love of Jesus and his followers.

We see then that the ongoing work of integration, of sanctification, of working out our salvation, requires that we take seriously the role of suffering in that process. Suffering in any dimension or domain that the mind/body/soul matrix occupies. God works in the presence of suffering because of its potential to drive us into ever more deeply connected relationship with the Holy Trinity and with our fellow believers.

As with Job, God does not explain our suffering; he *uses* it. We are the ones who want an explanation so that we can understand it and thereby control it, be in charge of it, like I want to be master over all of my life's circumstances. *I* want to be in charge, rather than trusting God to be in charge. Hence, my impulse is to avoid suffering at all costs.

And it is in these places of suffering that the glory we have explored in this book will be realized in its own particular way, not because suffering is God's idea or something in which he takes the slightest degree of delight. In many respects, suffering is a measurement not just of pain but rather of how broken our relationships are and how alone we are as a result. It is into that suffering that God relentlessly comes, not *primarily* to stop our suffering but to bring deep relationship. To the degree that suffering remains, so does God, ever at the ready to deepen our relationships even further with him and each other and so change our relationship with the suffering we endure.

Hope, then, is an outgrowth of the progression that this book has suggested, such that we need not fear suffering as we often do. While not pursuing it for any good reason of its own, we can truly rejoice in it as we are formed ever more durably and beautifully into the image of Jesus *in fully embodied and communal ways*, the only image into which we can be formed that will be able to withstand the beauty of the new heaven and earth that are coming.

But not everyone who suffers moves in the direction of integration, of wholeness, of joy in the face of their pain. For some, the work of revealing who they are brings them to a crisis point at which they cannot tolerate the intensity of being loved. At first glance, this would seem absurd. Who, when offered the opportunity to be seen, soothed, safe, and launched securely into new realms of beauty and goodness (yes, with the risk of being wounded, but also with the confidence of those wounds being cared for), would not want to do this? As it turns out, more people than you would think.

In fact, far many more avoid this work than the number

of those who choose to pick up their crosses. And not because they are cowards. Or are stupid. It is because this kind of work is very hard to do, given how much fear and shame encumber us. When Jesus spoke of a gate and then a path that is narrow with few who choose to travel it, he knew what he was talking about. Surely, I often find that path hard to choose myself.[1]

There have been more times than I would like to admit that patients have left treatment, either in individual psychotherapy or after having been part of a confessional community. Perhaps they reach a place where either the suffering they are enduring becomes too much or, even more significantly, they find themselves unable to tolerate the intimacy, the felt sense of exposure, of being seen by those who are coming to find and love them. They instead perceive these people to be coming to kill them. Not literally, of course. But with no less fear involved. Just as did Adam and Eve upon hearing God walking in the garden. And so they depart.

Sometimes this departure happens quickly, after only the first session with a patient or their first encounter with a confessional community. Other times it happens after weeks, months, or even years of work. But when it does, the relational mechanics of what is taking place are the same. The departure is a testimony to how that person has reached, at least for the time being, the limit of their capacity to hope.

Something has happened, whether it is obvious to them or not, that has brought them to a place where their fear of suffering outweighs their ability to hope and, more importantly, their ability to be in relationship with other people who can help them do so. People have all kinds of ways of exiting relationships when their fear of suffering outpaces their capacity to imagine how they will persevere in the face of it. And these fear-based exits are not limited to the psychotherapy consultation room.

We exit friendships. We exit marriages. We exit church relationships. Yes, of course, there are times when setting limits in relationships is necessary for survival, let alone flourishing. But that is not what I'm referring to here, and this is not the most common setting in which we leave, in which we find ourselves awash in hopelessness. Such exits are as common as they are ancient. Adam and Eve did it. Cain did it. Abram/ Abraham did it. Moses and David did it. In our fear, our shame, and our suffering, we exit into isolation, only to find our suffering enhanced.

One story in particular in which we see this tendency playing out is the encounter between Jesus and the rich lawyer whom we read about in three of the four Gospels. This is an interchange that has a great deal to say about what is at the heart of forming hope in the presence of suffering and what that hope leads to, as well as the necessary risks involved in forming it.

We can glean much from this story, including reflections about the place and role of wealth in our lives. But I would invite you here to consider that the affluence of the rich young ruler was but the surface manifestation of the deeper drama that unfolds in this story, a drama, as it turns out, that is as much about hope and suffering and the ease with which we cover over the latter in ways we are often unaware of. As we explore it, we will see that one thing in particular that stands out in this regard, and we see it only in the Gospel of Mark.[2]

In Mark's account in chapter 10, after the lawyer "ran up to

[Jesus] and fell on his knees before him," revealing the urgency of his quest, he asked, "'Good teacher . . . what must I do to inherit eternal life?'"

Although it is easy to dismiss any notion that this man was suffering, not least because of the comfort and protection provided by his wealth, we too often err in believing that this story is mostly or even only about money, unaware that our affluence also often covers a wealth, as it were, of our own suffering. We, like the rich young ruler, are hardly attuned to what our memories would reveal should we give them the opportunity and what our bodies often *do* reveal. Just consider our man of affluence here, whose urgent pace and posture declare what words could not fully say.

Moreover, it is possible for us to miss the significance of the lawyer's actual question. He wants *eternal* life. In the Hebrew tradition, the word translated "eternal" was not just or even mostly a measurement of time. Rather, it was a word used to describe the form or quality of life that one experiences.[3] To have eternal life was to have life with God, the nature of which was joy-filled, meaningful, and deep.

However, it appears that the lawyer assumes that having this way of life requires that *he* be the prime mover. *He* is responsible to prove that he is worthy of receiving this life, this love of God. Hence, "What must I do . . . ?" It seems to be inconceivable to him that *simply because he was alive* Jesus would want to offer him the life that he really wants.

The problem with this posture, of course, is that as long as I believe that in order for you to love me, I first must work to make myself worthy of your love, worthy of you, *I immediately and invariably disable myself, interpersonally and neurobiologically, from receiving it.* No matter how desperately I long to be seen, soothed, safe, and secure in your presence, if I primarily believe that my behavior at any time might permanently cut off my connection to you, my anxiety about this very possibility will make it virtually impossible for me to be open to receiving what I desperately long for from you. Then I will search all the harder for what might very well be right in front of me. This was the case for our lawyer friend.

In response, Jesus first notes that only God is good, a significant comment in and of itself, for indeed, only God is good enough to bear the necessary weight of the glory of relationships, and without his initiation and ever-present faithfulness, relationships will not survive. Then Jesus acknowledges the "what to do and what not to do" implicit in the attorney's query, referencing, generally, the latter portion of the Ten Commandments. A do and don't list.

You can sense Jesus testing the waters of the lawyer's intentions and capacity, essentially exploring how serious he is about moving into a real relationship with God. Testing him—mind you, with hopeful kindness—to see how far into intimacy, how deeply into eternal life this young man is willing to go.

The lawyer's response reveals how he thinks about the world. He answers Jesus by indicating that he has for his entire life checked all the boxes, working exceptionally hard to guarantee success in following Torah. For indeed, this is the only way he knows how to live. His wealth is the evidence that he is a hard worker—a hard worker at *everything*. Work that is likely driven by an insatiable longing to be enough. And so he strives to be enough by keeping each and every one of the commands that Jesus cites. A keeping that will ensure that God will be happy with him, that he will be loved.

In essence, what he does in business, he does in relationships. That is, he works hard at succeeding in everything and as such controls his own destiny. But this does not expel the ever-present, nagging anxiety that at any given moment, should he *not* check the right box, things might devolve before his very eyes, not least his relationship with God.

Perhaps when Jesus cites the Torah, the young man begins—but only begins—to infer validation and gain a rising confidence in his commitment to this way of being, this way of working hard to prove himself and compensate for his underlying sense of inadequacy. An inadequacy that lies hidden from his conscious awareness—and from the awareness of the disciples who are watching this drama unfold.

In this initial part of the dialogue, Jesus has set the stage for what follows. It appears, given the assumptions that we too are making of what is going on here, that Jesus is interested in outcomes. "You know the commandments . . ." implies, "Have you worked hard enough to prove yourself worthy?" Yet he is actually inviting the lawyer to take the risk of allowing Jesus to *love* him. With his next maneuver, Jesus pivots. And when he does, the lawyer loses his balance.

The text in Mark is almost jarring if we are paying attention. But if we are not, we may miss the moment when everything changes. In fact, we often miss it in our relationship with Jesus and with others who are trying to love us, just as the lawyer missed it. Nowhere else do we read what Mark writes: "Jesus looked at him *and loved him*" (10:21, italics mine). Given that Mark's Gospel is well known for moving at a rapid pace, providing the reader with the most important things the writer wanted to say—brief and to the point without unnecessary detail—it is striking that he includes this sentence.

Mark captured what we have been exploring over the course of this book—the way we most powerfully experience what it means to be loved through what we sense in our bodies, not least through nonverbal cues coming from others such as eye contact and facial expression. This interaction is important in our story here. Something about Jesus's *look* captured the attention of the writer. Something about Jesus's look that the writer saw, that *someone* saw—but that the lawyer missed. Or if he didn't miss it, the look undid him.

It was the look of love. A look that we are all watching for. But a look that, when it finds us, is able to touch the parts of us that we have been trying our entire lives to bury, to hide, hoping we can just be rid of them. Parts we hate. Parts that feel as if shame has taken up residence on entire floors, let alone a few rooms in the houses of our souls. Parts we cover over with thick walls of concrete.

The intimacy that Paul implies in his language of faith and justification and peace with God that all lead to our sharing in God's glory was found in Jesus's look. The same look that we would not be surprised to find that Paul encountered on the road to Damascus. This look of love, uncompromising, unflinching, is coming for us unapologetically. And as much as we long to be loved, we also are terrified by what *we, in our implicit memory, interpret it to represent* when it finds us.

We work as hard as we can to cope with our lives in the wake of our traumas and shame, having figured out all the tactics that we need to employ to get God to love us, because in the primal recesses of our bones, we still believe we are at war with God. And those warring parts are terrified of intimacy because they remember that our traumas were born in the context of intimacy.

And for some of us, that intimacy is deeply tied to people who were supposed to be the safest people for us on the planet. Our parents. Our siblings. Our teachers and coaches. Or the man I'm dating. Or the woman I'm married to. Or my boss. Or the church, which ends up being a euphemism for individual people with real names, pastors or elders or other members of Jesus's body with whom we have worshiped at one time or another and who have hurt us. Those who used their place in the institution to cope with their own unfinished emotional and spiritual business, in the process leaving our bodies and souls in their wake.

That look of being wanted, of being desired without being consumed; of being seen, soothed, safe, and secure—*that* look, we worry, can come with the potential for painful negative side effects. But that was the look Jesus was willing to offer if it meant yet one more young Jewish man would take the risk of running for daylight when it flashed into his darkness.

With hope bound up in that look, Jesus proceeds. "One thing you lack." Which, we might guess, would have heightened, if only briefly, our lawyer's anticipation that Jesus was going to reveal something that he didn't yet have *but that he could work to acquire.*

Perhaps he imagined that Jesus was about to give him an insight, yes, but then go on to give him a task, something *else* he could "do" to guarantee the life with God he wanted, just as he had worked so hard to acquire all his other possessions.

We can sense for the briefest moment the lawyer's heart rate accelerating, as he anticipated that he was about to receive the answer to the question he had been asking his entire life. The water to quench his thirst. He was standing on the threshold of hope.

And then, crushing disappointment. His hopes dashed. The swell of grief. "Go, sell everything you have and give to the poor, and you will have treasure in heaven. Then come, follow me."[4] Notice the irony in Jesus's words. He points out that the lawyer *lacks* something. But how is this even possible, and what could it be? He has *everything*.

Everything, that is, except a relationship with someone—anyone, perhaps—and in this case, Jesus, who at this stage of the game only wants the young man to be *with* him. The one thing—a relationship—for which he *didn't have to* work. For which, in fact, he *couldn't* work.

Jesus didn't need the man's hard work. He didn't need his money. As I have mentioned, and as the disciples inquired immediately after this interchange, it is easy for us to assume this story is mostly or even only about wealth. I'm not so sure.

I am inviting you to consider that underneath the attention to wealth, this is a story about how we build elaborate coping strategies over which we wield tight-fisted control to protect ourselves from our traumas and our shame. Jesus was not merely telling the ruler to give up his wealth because, in and of itself, it was "bad" or merely because it was an idol, which, by the end of the story, it appears to have been. Rather, his wealth represented the young man's insistence on working hard to prove himself worthy of being loved.

Simultaneously, the young man's wealth was the physical

reality that protected him from the vulnerability required for him to receive that very love. To give up his wealth was to operate without a net, opening himself to love without being able to control all the variables that would ensure that this love would last.

Selling all he had would be an act of great vulnerability, not just because he would no longer be wealthy but because it would expose how relationally poor he was. And what if, in the end, no one came to make sure he was seen, soothed, safe, and secure? He could not guarantee a positive outcome, because he had little practice forming hope for his life in this way, as is the case for many of us.

But Jesus's look was intended to let the young man know beyond words that Jesus could *see* him and wanted the man to be *with* him. Intended to communicate what words are often unable to accomplish, it was a look that met the man where he was—as one whose hope was centered in himself alone, in his own effort to be "okay" in the world—and brought him into a place of beauty and goodness. This place in which the man's obedience to God's desires for his behavior as expressed in the law would emerge as an expression of love and gratitude. This obedience would no longer come from fear that he would be found to be inadequate, as he believed himself to be. And indeed, his hope could be only *in himself* because he was not yet able to imagine hope to be found anywhere outside his own agency.

Of course, we cannot know the workings of the young man's inner life with absolute certainty. But the gospel writer's attention to the detail of Jesus's gaze, matched against the ruler's response, tells us something vital. The man's posture toward relationships, it appears, was one overly dominated by a left-brained manner of attuning to the world. One that sees the world as an object to be observed from a distance and then manipulated to reduce one's distress on one's own terms, by oneself. It experiences the world as being something from which I am separate rather than something I am "with" and that wants to be "with" me.

We sense this posture, this embodied conviction of who God is (a scorekeeper with whom the lawyer believes he is still at war) and how God sees him (an inadequate man who has yet to measure up), a posture that he has been maintaining most of his life, given his accumulation of wealth at a young age. From this posture Jesus seeks to deliver him.

In fact, Jesus is attempting to move the attorney into a more balanced, more integrated state of mind. He wants to move him from a place of *talking about* eternal life to a place of *being with* Eternal Life—with Jesus. He hopes that the young man will see him looking at him with love and permit himself to feel seen.

But it is possible that the man was so encased in his own protective armor that he *could not* see Jesus seeing him. Or, just as likely, it is possible that Jesus's look undid him. It is possible that the lawyer could not tolerate Jesus's gaze. For indeed, for many of us, no matter our social status, the look of anyone who intends to come to find us with lovingkindness may evoke within us as much distress as comfort. For, depending on any number of variables, to be seen can feel as threatening as it feels healing.

And so we read, "At this the man's face fell. He went away

sad, because he had great wealth."⁵ His face fell. He could not hold Jesus's look. To give up his wealth would mean he would open all the doors to all the rooms of his soul that held his shame and his unresolved traumas, whatever they were. And the fear of what he presumed would be the suffering waiting for him therein was too much. He did not yet have enough neural real estate that correlated with a confident sense of the presence of others—of the Other—to enable him to hope that Jesus would come through. And thus he left with, and in, his grief.

◆ ◆ ◆

In Paul's final words of our passage from Romans, found at the beginning of this chapter, we discover that we have come full circle. In fact, the entire passage functions much like a repeating cycle that draws us ever more maturely into the wisdom that emerges within us from being in relationship with Jesus and his followers. Thus, we continue to journey deeper and deeper into our suffering on the way to forming hope that leads us to yet the next, weightier encounter with God's glory. Not unlike the figure below.

How does our encounter with this story from Mark's Gospel reflect what we have been walking through over the course of this book? What does it have to say to the people we have met in these pages about the nature of suffering, about what it means to persevere, about the building of character that leads to hope that never, ever disappoints us, never puts us to shame? How do the words of our passage from Romans reflect what is happening between Jesus and the rich young ruler?

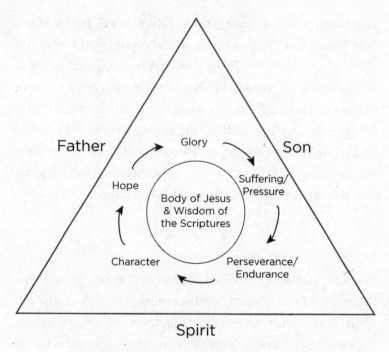

Empowered by the Spirit;
in the presence of the Body of Jesus;
informed by the wisdom of the Scriptures.

As we have seen from the lives of the people in previous chapters, suffering takes many forms, far more than one could ever count. And we all have our strategies for coping with it. Coping, that is, until we can't.

For those of us whose lives seem absent of any significant degree of suffering, the story of the rich young ruler reminds us, in the words of my friends Katherine and Jay Wolf, that we all have disabilities. Some are just more visible than others. And for those who have read this while swimming in a sea of suffering, even we have our tactics that we employ that enable us to live, if not well, then adequately enough to get by.

Regardless of where we find ourselves on the spectrum, no matter how obvious or hidden our suffering, mostly we just want relief. From our pain. From our suffering. We're not even aware that what we're looking for is a look from Jesus. Often we have such little experience knowing that this is what our body and soul are really searching for that we certainly don't always know to ask for or expect it. We're simply looking for relief, usually on our own terms.

And Jesus comes to us offering that relief, though usually, as with our wealthy friend, *not* on our terms. He meets us where we are, just as we are—just as he met the wealthy man where he was, acknowledging the way he was used to navigating the world—with all of our props, addictions, and resentment toward the ways our traumas have happened and have not been healed. But Jesus refuses to leave us there—instead, he *looks* at us. With love.

Yet our stories, replete as they are with memories of bygone wounds in the context of intimacy, at times have difficulty holding his gaze. For as much as we long to be seen by him, parts of us are fearful of where he will then ask us to go. Fearful of what it will mean to follow him into all the rooms in our house where the remaining detritus of our brokenness—and that of preceding generations—is to be found.

We have seen how, in God's relational and new-creational economy, the suffering with which we come to Jesus—suffering that we hope he will eliminate fully and forever—may actually be something that remains with us for the rest of our lives. Granted, it will change its form, and with these changes our relationship with suffering will be transformed as we are made more and more into the image of Jesus.

We, like the woman with a bleeding disorder in Mark's Gospel, thought that the healing of our suffering was a one-step process, only to find out that Jesus has every intention of walking with us into every corner of our interior and embodied lives, taking as much time as it will take to transform us fully into the outposts of beauty and goodness he imagines we are becoming.[6]

For indeed, as Jesus looked at the rich young ruler with love, it was glory that he saw. Jesus was looking into a realm that no one else could see, one in which he saw the vision of who that man was to become as he bore the weight of glory that, with Jesus's gaze, he was beginning to bear. The gaze of joy, of pride, of jubilant hospitality in anticipation of yet another one of God's sons and daughters opening himself to the love of the King.

But as we have seen, the work of being receptive to Jesus's look is very, very hard.

Jesus does not disagree that the work involved—being receptive to love so as to transform one's suffering into glorious, joyful relationship by perseverance in the presence of vulnerable community—is indeed very, very hard. Harder, in fact, than for a camel to pass through the eye of a needle. Hard enough, in fact, that many of us find it too overwhelming, too frightening, too close to exposing the suffering we have either quietly or openly endured for so long.

When we get to that point, some of us, like our lawyer friend, exit our relationships. With Jesus. With others. And with parts of ourselves that were ever so close to the love they thought they saw in the look.

But Jesus does not leave us alone. He does not leave you, the reader, alone. As he reminded the disciples and so also reminds us: no matter what our stories have been—no matter the depth of our traumas and shame, no matter how impossible it seems to imagine a life in which the suffering you've endured and are enduring will ever be any different—hope is waiting to be formed.

We cannot form it on our own, for as Jesus also reminds us, "With man this is impossible . . ."[7] It was impossible for the attorney and, for that matter, any of the people you have met in these pages—and for you and for me—to form hope on our own. But we are not doing this alone. And we are not forming hope around an ideology or a job or a church or a theology or a political philosophy or our economy.

We are forming our hope as the result of being loved by Jesus. As the result of our real time-and-space embodied encounters with his look, his body language, his tone of voice, his reimagining and retelling of the stories of trauma that we have believed for so long are fixed in our history and our remembered reality. Jesus forms our hope through the power of his love that has been poured out into our hearts through the Holy Spirit who has been joyfully given to us, whose delight is to occupy space in our hearts. *He* is the one who is loving us into hope, remaining with us as we persevere on this long road of life, which is full of the suffering in which we come to rejoice because of the secure attachment we have to him and to his people.

And so we come to the end of our text, and the end of this exploration of suffering and the formation of hope. And yet we are also at the beginning. The beginning of the next part of our story, yours and mine together, which will, in all confidence, grow into the fullness of the beauty and goodness we are destined to become, repeatedly moving from glory to suffering to perseverance to character to hope—and back again to the glory that God ordained from before the foundation of the world.

No matter how hard the road is, I am confident that as we co-labor in the power and presence of the Holy Spirit to create and curate that which we have been given to steward, Jesus will bring to completion that which he has begun.

And that, my friend, no matter how hard the suffering, is something in which we can hope.

ACKNOWLEDGMENTS

In many respects, when considering the expression of gratitude for all who have been involved in bringing a book project into the hands of you who hold it, the list of people to thank, though not limitless, is nonetheless lengthy. In fact, I can't even name all for whom gratitude is well deserved, but here are those who immediately come to mind, and who I'm confident don't get paid well enough for their presence and support.

I begin with Carolyn McCready, who, over several years—and long before she became my editor—embodied deeply interested curiosity and support for the writing and speaking work that I do at the intersection of neuroscience and Christian spiritual formation. She was, moreover, unabashed in her enthusiasm for this project in particular, and I have been grateful for her kindness and generosity of spirit as we labored together over what have become the pages you are reading. It is no secret that the best editors simultaneously serve as part-time psychotherapists for the writers with whom they work, given how maddeningly prone to self-doubt we writers can sometimes be. Carolyn, without question, for me held both roles with grace and skill, providing the necessary balance of affirmation and direction where needed. And for this I am particularly humbled and grateful.

I am aware that the entire team at Zondervan who has been involved in this project deserve more thanks than I will be able to offer here. It is such a lovely thing to be wanted, and from the beginning of this process I have felt nothing other than that. Moreover, I have sensed this in my interactions with everyone who has laid eyes on this book's conceptual and editorial journey. As is true for most authors, how any book I write presents itself in its physical appearance matters to me a great deal. A book is not simply a collection of words on pages; I long for the very material that holds and offers the words to be in itself an expression of what is contained therein. This too has been an important element of this project for which the team has provided great care and consideration.

As I have approached and completed this manuscript, I have been deeply aware of the ongoing support of the people with whom I work most closely, including my executive assistant, Jodi Witmer; my social media director, Kara Yuza; and my cohosts and producers of the *Being Known* podcast, Pepper Sweeney and Amy Cella. And then there is Leslie Nunn Reed, whose many decades of support as my friend and literary agent have been immeasurably valuable, and to whom this book is dedicated.

There is nothing I write or speak about that is not first discovered and exercised in the company of my fellow colleagues in our practice at New Story Behavioral Health, along with the patients that we serve. I am deeply humbled that I have had the privilege of working alongside such a kind, gifted group of clinicians, and in the presence of those who are willing to do the very hard work of telling more truly to and with us the stories of their suffering that lead to glory.

As I say every time I have the opportunity, I don't deserve my life, and there is no greater evidence of this than that of my marriage to Phyllis. It is her patient, faithful presence that continues to provide the hard deck that enables me to do this work—work that only continues to expand the joy of following Jesus—and to bear witness to his kingdom that is here and is coming in its fullness.

NOTES

INTRODUCTION

1. Whereas an Eastern view of suffering responds by emptying one's mind of desire, so as to minimize its frustration, a Western approach seeks to mitigate suffering by overcoming it altogether. Neither posture imagines that suffering is actually to be used as part of what enables us to become more wholly human.

2. For a full exploration of this emerging phenomenon, see Jean Twenge, *iGen: Why Today's Super-Connected Kids Are Growing Up Less Rebellious, More Tolerant, Less Happy—and Completely Unprepared for Adulthood—and What That Means for the Rest of Us* (New York: Simon & Schuster, 2017).

3. Romans 1:20.

4. Psalm 13:1.

5. Colossians 1:27.

CHAPTER 1: JUST FAITH

1. Leo Tolstoy, *Anna Karenina* (New York: Penguin, 2000), 1.

2. Aidan Nichols, *A Key to Balthasar* (London: Darton, Longman & Todd, 2001), 1–9. I highlight this in *The Soul of Desire: Discovering the Neuroscience of Longing, Beauty, and Community* (Downers Grove, IL: InterVarsity Press, 2021), 42–43. Von

Balthasar does not address neuroscience per se, but I suggest that his insights are reflective of the general although overly simple notion that the brain operates "bottom to top, then right to left."

3. Antonio Damasio, *The Feeling of What Happens* (New York: Harcourt, 1999), 279–83.

4. Daniel J. Siegel, *The Developing Mind*, 2nd ed. (New York: Guilford, 2012), 367–68.

5. Attachment is the interpersonal interaction between a child and parent by which the immature child's brain utilizes the more mature parent's brain to help organize itself. The baby looks to the mother or father in order for the parent to help the baby regulate his or her emotional/physical distress. Research in this area describes secure and insecure forms of the attachment process, each of which has high correlation with various ways the brain of the child develops, and subsequently, how we function in relationships as adults. For more information, see Siegel, *Developing Mind*, 91–93.

6. Galatians 5:22–23.

7. The process of being seen, soothed, safe, and secure was first described by Dan Siegel and Tina Payne Bryson. Known as the 4 S's, they are words that together capture the essence of how secure attachment develops. I address an alternative way of using the word "secure" in *Soul of Desire*. For exploration of both, see Daniel J. Siegel and Tina Payne Bryson, *The Power of Showing Up* (New York: Ballantine, 2020), 5–6; and Thompson, *Soul of Desire*, 31–33.

8. N. T. Wright, *Paul for Everyone: Romans, Part 1* (Louisville: Westminster John Knox, 2004), 80–85.

9. N. T. Wright, *Justification* (Downers Grove, IL: InterVarsity Press, 2009), 117.

10. Anne Halley, personal comment and correspondence.

11. Pat Ogden, Kekuni Minton, and Clare Pain, *Trauma and the Body* (New York: Norton, 2006), 26–40.

12. George Grouios, Klio Semoglou, and Constantinos Chatzinikolaou, "The Effect of Simulated Mental Practice Technique on Free Throw Shooting Accuracy of Highly Skilled Basketball Players," *Journal of Human Movement Studies* 33.3 (January 1997): 119–38.

13. For more detailed exploration of the way confessional communities function, see Thompson, *Soul of Desire*, 91–112.

14. Earned secure attachment is that pattern of attachment that one can form as an adult by "making coherent sense" of the parts of one's story that represent unhealed wounds or unresolved trauma. This is one of the primary goals of all relational healing endeavors. For greater exploration, see Daniel J. Siegel and Mary Hartzell, *Parenting from the Inside Out* (New York: Tarcher, 2003), 126–27, 143–47.

CHAPTER 2: A DECLARATION OF WAR— AND PEACE

1. John Goldingay, *Old Testament Theology* (Downers Grove, IL: InterVarsity Press, 2003), 131–35. Goldingay emphasizes that subtlety and innuendo worked to overthrow the creation. It is so often the case that shame's power derives from its very subtlety.

2. Goldingay, *Old Testament Theology*, 131.

3. We are not told directly how it is that Eve comes to add her own edits to God's command in Genesis 2:15–17, that she and Adam ". . . must not touch it, or you will die."

4. Gaurav Patki, Ankita Salvi, Hesong Liu, and Samina Salim, "Witnessing Traumatic Events and Post-Traumatic Stress Disorder: Insights from an Animal Model," *Neuroscience Letters* 600 (July 23, 2015): 28–32. The witnessing of trauma occurs in various degrees of severity, from our embarrassment with another's embarrassment to bearing witness to severe acts of physical violence.

5. I explore this in detail in *The Soul of Shame: Retelling the Stories*

We Believe about Ourselves (Downers Grove, IL: InterVarsity Press, 2015), 100–107.

6. Genesis 3:6.

7. Genesis 3:7.

8. Genesis 3:5.

9. John Gottman is considered one of the foremost researchers on the topic of marriage and romantic relationships. He pioneered work that emphasized, among many things, the role that contempt plays in the long-term survival of a marriage. See John Gottman, *Why Marriages Succeed or Fail* (New York: Simon & Schuster, 1995).

10. Sue Johnson, *Hold Me Tight* (New York: Little, Brown, 2008).

11. David Carrasco, *Religions of Mesoamerica*, 2nd ed. (Long Grove, IL: Waveland Press, 2014), 25–26, 66–67.

12. Ephesians 6:12.

13. Matthew 11:25–30.

14. Jim Wilder, *Renovated* (Colorado Springs: NavPress, 2020), 6–8.

15. "Japanese Holdout," Wikipedia, https://en.wikipedia.org/wiki /Japanese_holdout.

16. Here again we are emphasizing the role of the 4 S's: being seen, soothed, safe, and secure.

17. Mark Wolynn, *It Didn't Start with You* (New York: Penguin, 2017), 25–39.

18. See Richard Schwartz, *Internal Family Systems Therapy*, 2nd ed. (New York: Guilford, 2020).

19. Alison Cook and Kimberly Miller, *Boundaries for Your Soul* (Nashville: Thomas Nelson, 2018).

20. Psalm 42:5.

CHAPTER 3: A WIDE PLACE TO STAND

1. Pat Ogden, Kekuni Minton, and Clare Pain, *Trauma and the Body* (New York: Norton, 2006), 206–10.

2. Genesis 2:7 reminds us that God began with dust into which he breathed the breath of life such that we became living beings.

He began with our physicality. Our bodies are thus sequenced first in our becoming human. This does not make them more important, but it does highlight their place in the process of creation, and then new creation.

3. Luke 24:13–35. N. T. Wright, *Luke for Everyone* (Louisville: Westminster John Knox, 2004), 291–98; William Barclay, *The Gospel of Luke*, rev. ed. (Philadelphia: Westminster, 1975), 293–96.

4. Romans 5:2a.

5. See Francine Shapiro, *Eye Movement Desensitization and Reprocessing Therapy* (New York: Guilford, 2018). EMDR (eye movement desensitization and reprocessing) is now a commonly employed psychotherapeutic intervention that is recognized to reduce intense and overwhelming emotional distress, especially in the presence of post-traumatic stress disorders (PTSD).

6. See *The Paradigm*, BibleProject Podcast series, episodes 2–5, https://bibleproject.com/podcast/series/paradigm/.

7. Daniel J. Siegel, *The Developing Mind*, 2nd ed. (New York: Guilford, 2012), 367–68.

8. See Bessel van der Kolk, *The Body Keeps the Score* (New York: Penguin, 2015). Van der Kolk underscores the role of the body in our experience of trauma and its healing. It remains, however, that science only ever describes the mechanics of how the material world operates; it does not provide meaning for those mechanics.

9. As with all the Scriptures, it is helpful to read multiple translations to capture the fullness of the content of this psalm, not least vv. 7–8, to which I am paying most attention.

CHAPTER 4: GLORY

1. Aidan Nichols, *A Key to Balthasar* (London: Darton, Longman, and Todd, 2011), 2–3.

2. Psalm 19:1.

3. Exodus 33:18.

4. 1 Chronicles 16:24; 29:11.

5. Isaiah 6:3; 63:1.

6. Habakkuk 2:14.

7. 1 Corinthians 6:20; 10:31.

8. Lesslie Newbigin, *The Light Has Come* (Grand Rapids: Eerdmans, 1982), 225.

9. John 15:16.

10. John 1:14; 2 Corinthians 4:6; Hebrews 1:3.

11. Newbigin, *Light Has Come*, 225.

12. Philippians 2:6–11.

13. John 17:1.

14. John 3:17.

15. Newbigin, *Light Has Come*, 226.

16. Hebrews 2:10.

17. Luke 3:22.

18. Luke 9:28–36.

19. Daniel J. Siegel and Tina Payne Bryson, *The Power of Showing Up* (New York: Ballantine, 2020), 5–6.

20. 2 Corinthians 4:17.

21. C. S. Lewis, *The Weight of Glory: And Other Addresses* (New York: HarperCollins, 1980), 38.

22. Colossians 3:3.

23. John 1:14 KJV.

24. John 21:7.

CHAPTER 5: SUFFERING: THE STORY OF THE PRESENT AGE

1. See N. T. Wright, *Paul and the Faithfulness of God* (Minneapolis: Fortress, 2013). Wright throughout this work not only explores Paul's theology but provides a rich background of Paul's plausible life story and the multiple forces of his world that shaped him.

2. Regarding "parts" that are addressed in the psychotherapy model of internal family systems, see Alison Cook and Kimberly

Miller, *Boundaries for Your Soul* (Nashville: Thomas Nelson, 2018), 219.

3. Scott Peck, *The Road Less Traveled* (New York: Touchstone/ Simon & Schuster, 1978), 15.

4. Matthew 9:20–22; Mark 5:25–34; Luke 8:43–48.

5. An exceedingly short list includes C. S. Lewis, *The Problem of Pain* and *A Grief Observed*; Viktor Frankl, *Man's Search for Meaning*; Nancy Guthrie, *Be Still, My Soul*; Philip Yancey, *Where Is God When It Hurts?*; Nicholas Wolterstorff, *Lament for a Son*; Diane Langberg, *Suffering and the Heart of God*; Sheldon Vanauken, *A Severe Mercy*; Katherine and Jay Wolf, *Suffer Strong*.

6. One would also include those literary works of fiction that have brought suffering into sharp relief like few other media can. For example, Leo Tolstoy's *Anna Karenina*.

7. Jeremiah 6:16 NRSVue.

8. John 16:33.

9. This is not to be confused with abandonment as understood by existential philosophers such as Heidegger or Sartre. For more on this, see "Abandonment (Existentialism)," https://en.wikipedia .org/wiki/Abandonment_(existentialism). Moreover, I am not here offering a robust exploration of anxiety as we express it culturally, nor its various neurophysiological correlates. For that, see Joseph LeDoux, *Anxious: Using the Brain to Understand and Treat Fear and Anxiety* (New York: Penguin, 2016).

10. Genesis 2:18.

11. C. S. Lewis, *The Great Divorce* (New York: HarperCollins, 1973), 10.

12. Curt Thompson, *The Soul of Desire* (Downers Grove, IL: InterVarsity Press, 2021), 21–33.

13. Allan Schore, *Affect Regulation* (New York: Norton, 2003), 37–52.

14. Curt Thompson, *Anatomy of the Soul* (Carol Stream, IL: Tyndale, 2010), 63–87.

15. From Donald Hebb, Canadian neuropsychologist from whose work was coined the saying, "Neurons that fire together, wire together." This suggests that the more frequently a sequence of

neurons fire in the same pattern, that pattern becomes more permanent and more easily activated. This is the fundamental basis of how we come to encode memories that can be retrieved.

16. These include the *conscious, vertical, horizontal, memory, narrative, state, interpersonal, temporal,* and *transpirational* domains. For more detail see Daniel J. Siegel, *Mindsight,* 2nd ed. (New York: Bantam, 2010), 71–75.

17. David Sbarra and James A. Coan, "Theory, Method, and Prediction in the Psychophysiology of Relationships," *International Journal of Psychophysiology* 88 (2013): 219–23.

18. Matthew 12:32; Mark 10:30.

19. 1 Corinthians 2:6–8.

20. N. T. Wright, *Paul for Everyone: Romans, Part 1* (Louisville: Westminster John Knox, 2004), 140–41.

21. C. S. Lewis, *The Voyage of the Dawn Treader* (New York: Harper Trophy, 1980), 112–18.

22. John 5:1–14.

23. John 8:2–11.

24. See Hope Heals for Katherine and Jay Wolf's story and the ministry of beauty and goodness that has emerged (https://www.hopeheals.com/).

25. Romans 8:17; Philippians 3:10; 1 Peter 4:13–16.

CHAPTER 6: PERSEVERANCE

1. Gerald May, *Addiction and Grace* (New York: HarperCollins, 2007), 4.

2. 2 Corinthians 4:16.

3. Luke 4:13.

4. Matthew 27:46.

5. See Psalm 22. Note the turn in the entire theme of the poem at verse 19.

6. See Matthew 26:53.

7. See Acts 9. Paul's encounter with Ananias bears witness that

from the moment of Paul's encounter with Jesus on the road to Damascus, he was in need of the support of others, not to mention that his missionary journeys were always ones in which he was accompanied by fellow believers.

8. Numbers 20.

9. Numbers 12:3; Deuteronomy 34:10.

10. Curt Thompson, *Anatomy of the Soul* (Carol Stream, IL: Tyndale, 2010), 152–54.

11. Luke 22:31–32.

12. Mark 16:7.

13. Thompson, *Anatomy of the Soul*, 226–28.

14. Todd Billings, *Rejoicing in Lament* (Grand Rapids: Brazos, 2015).

15. See Dr. Elizabeth Hall with Curt Thompson, MD, "Loving and Losing," *NeuroFaith* podcast.

16. Liz Hall, "Professor of Psychology Liz Hall Shares Her Breast Cancer Survival Story," Biola University, October 15, 2018, www.facebook.com/watch/?v=289267055019077.

17. See The Bible Project, "The Book of Numbers Overview," https://bibleproject.com/explore/video/numbers/.

18. See 1 Kings 18–19 for a picture of how quickly Elijah's posture toward his calling changed between his confrontation with the prophets of Baal and that with Jezebel.

19. Daniel J. Siegel, *Pocket Guide to Interpersonal Neurobiology* (New York: Norton, 2012), 41.4–6.

20. Research currently demonstrates at least the following that enhance neuroplasticity: proper sleep, proper diet, aerobic exercise, mindfulness practices, creative novelty, humor, deep reading, and deeply attached, growing human relationships.

21. Psalm 90:4; 2 Peter 3:8.

22. Babette Rothschild, *8 Keys to Safe Trauma Recovery* (New York: Norton, 2010), 34, 60–62.

23. Psalm 22; Matthew 27:46.

24. Philippians 3:10–11.

CHAPTER 7: CHARACTER

1. See, for instance, Joseph and his brothers, Genesis 37; and Judah and Tamar, Genesis 38.

2. See Nicholas Carr, *The Shallows* (New York: Norton, 2011), for a detailed exploration of the impact of the internet on our attentional capacity.

3. William Barclay, *The Letter to the Romans* (Philadelphia: Westminster, 1975), 74.

4. John 15:16.

5. 2 Corinthians 3:18.

6. Scott Buckhout sermon, Restoration Anglican Church, Arlington, Virginia, August 21, 2022. See this helpful synopsis provided by a sermon delivered by Scott Buckhout in which he highlighted how we are nourished by the Spirit, the Scriptures, and the body of Jesus, all of which move us in the direction of deepening our character as we are continually more deeply persuaded of the place and power of Jesus in the world and in our lives and how that leads to the bearing of fruit. https:// restorationarlington.org/sermons/.

7. "The Tale of Two Trees," BibleProject Podcast, *Tree of Life*, episode 3, January 20, 2020, https://bibleproject.com/podcast /tale-two-trees/.

8. "How Do You Read the Bible?," BibleProject Podcast, *The Paradigm*, episode 1, September 13, 2021, https://bibleproject .com/podcast/how-do-you-read-bible/.

9. For example, Potter's Inn Soul Care Institute; The Transforming Center; Apprentice Institute for Christian Spiritual Formation; Coracle.

10. Ephesians 4:15–16.

11. Daniel J. Siegel, *Mindsight* (New York: Bantam, 2010), 70–71.

12. Romans 8:29; 2 Corinthians 3:18.

13. On multiple occasions in Deuteronomy 8 Moses commands the people of Israel to "remember" and to be sure not to "forget" Yahweh, saying, "If you ever forget the LORD your God and follow other gods and worship and bow down to them, I testify against you today that you will surely be destroyed" (8:19).

14. Lawrence K. Low and Hwai-Jong Cheng, "Axon Pruning: An Essential Step Underlying the Developmental Plasticity of Neuronal Connections," *Philosophical Transactions of the Royal Society B: Biological Sciences* 361.1473 (July 23, 2006): 1531–44, doi 10.1098/rstb.2006.1883.

15. Allan Schore, "A Neuropsychoanalytic Viewpoint," *Psychoanalytic Dialogues* 15.6 (2005): 829–54.

16. Daniel J. Siegel, *The Developing Mind*, 2nd ed. (New York: Bantam, 2010), 104–11.

17. Strangely enough, this even holds true in a setting in which the child is only being offered food and clothing with no additional emotional or relational support. Even *those* acts on the parts of adults have their origin *not* in the prefrontal cortical, planning part of the adult's brain, which rationally thinks, "I should feed this child because it's the right thing to do." Rather, they come from the lower, mid-brain, and right-hemispheric regions of their brains—meaning essentially that they emerge first from neural networks highly correlated with primary emotional states, states that are the seedbed for attachment. The fact that even in emotionally barren settings children are still given food and shelter of some kind means they are not being treated fully as if they were merely a chair. Such nourishment begins with relational/emotional attachment that is expressed in embodied form.

18. Ed Tronick, *The Neurobehavioral and Social-Emotional Development of Infants and Children* (New York: Norton, 2007), 177–94.

19. For a more detailed exploration of attachment patterns, see Siegel, *Mindsight*, 166–89.

20. See Daniel J. Siegel and Tina Payne Bryson, *The Power of Showing Up* (New York: Ballantine, 2020), 5–6; and Curt Thompson, *The Soul of Desire* (Downers Grove, IL: InterVarsity Press, 2021), 31–33.

21. Daniel J. Siegel, *The Mindful Therapist* (New York: Norton, 2010), 101–19. Note in particular Siegel's metaphor of the "tripod of awareness" and the development of becoming more open, more observant, and ultimately more objective in one's awareness of the world. In this case, "objective" is not vis-à-vis "subjective," but rather, with greater openness, one can become more observant (rather than condemning) and thus able to see more of the entire object of one's life.

22. Colossians 3:3.

23. Karl Menninger, *Bulletin of the Menninger Clinic* 48.4–6 (September 1, 1984): 457.

24. John 4:1–42.

25. John 4:34.

26. John 19:30.

27. John 15:1–2.

28. You may be familiar with the marshmallow experiment with young children. Although those experiments do not have any direct correlation with predicting behavior as adults, the videotaped recordings of children struggling mightily—and often effectively!—demonstrate just how hard it is for us to delay gratification. See this re-creation of a test designed by Walter Mischel, PhD, Stanford University: "The Marshmallow Experiment—Instant Gratification," FloodSanDiego, www.youtube.com/watch?v=Yo4WF3cSd9Q.

29. See Mark 8:23; Luke 22:39–44; John 6:14–15.

30. Hebrews 12:1–2.

31. Daniel J. Siegel and Mary Hartzell, *Parenting from the Inside Out* (New York: Tarcher, 2003), 185–94.

32. In chapter 1 we briefly explored the window of tolerance, or a way to measure our capacity to withstand distressing

emotional experiences. To widen the window is to expand that capacity and make room for greater resilience.

33. Bonnie Badenoch, *Being a Brain-Wise Therapist* (New York: Norton, 2008), 100–101.

CHAPTER 8: HOPE

1. Daniel J. Siegel, *The Developing Mind*, 2nd ed. (New York: Guilford, 2012), 46–51, 71–74.
2. Barak Obama, "The Audacity of Hope," Democratic National Convention, Boston, Massachusetts, 2004, "Barak Obama Speech at the National Convention," C-SPAN, www.youtube.com/watch?v=eWynt87PaJ0.
3. Tom Holland, *Rubicon* (New York: Anchor, 2005), 177.
4. For example, Psalm 31:23–24; 37:9; 38:15; 42:5; Jeremiah 17:13; 1 Corinthians 13:13; 1 Timothy 4:10.
5. Tom Holland, *In the Shadow of the Sword* (New York: Anchor, 2012), 270–77.
6. Lesslie Newbigin, *Proper Confidence* (Grand Rapids: Eerdmans, 1995), 45–64.
7. See Arthur Brooks, "A Conservative's Plea: Let's Work Together," TED, April 6, 2016, www.youtube.com/watch?v=87AEeLpodnE.
8. See Steven Pinker, *The Better Angels of Our Nature* (New York: Penguin, 2011). Pinker argues that, relatively speaking, we are morally nobler and thus less violent now than we were in the past.
9. One need only observe the violence of shame, often transported via the mechanism of social media or in embodied action, with which we at times respond to the economic oppression and racism that we experience in our society.
10. Suniya S. Luthar, "The Culture of Affluence: Psychological Costs of Material Wealth," *Child Development* 74.6 (2003): 1581–93.
11. Note that another way to declare that one feels *unsafe* is to say

that one feels *afraid*. There is not space here to explore the implications of the difference in our usage of these two words (and the way many use the words "unsafe" or "I don't feel safe" has indeed changed dramatically in the last decade), but suffice to say that the use of the phrase "I don't feel safe" often carries with it the implication that the speaker has little to no agency to change what they feel. In saying these words in this way, their fear is reinforced.

12. Crystal Smith, Andrew Allen, and Lee Kannis-Dymand, "Social Media May Contribute to Eco-Distress: The Role of Nature-Relatedness as Both Causal Mechanism and Protective Factor," *Ecopsychology* 14.1 (March 8, 2022): 17–29, doi 10.1089/eco.2021.0020.

13. See The Perception Gap, https://perceptiongap.us/.

14. Michael Scherer, Ashley Parker, and Tyler Pager, "Historians Privately Warn Biden That America's Democracy Is Teetering," *Washington Post*, August 11, 2022, www.washingtonpost.com/politics/2022/08/10/biden-us-historians-democracy-threat/.

15. Flannery O'Connor, "The Novelist and the Believer," in *Mystery and Manners: Occasional Prose* (New York: Farrar, Straus and Giroux, 1970), 167.

16. See "Millennials and Gen Z Are More Anxious Than Previous Generations: Here's Why," *Folio*, University of Alberta, January, 28, 2020, www.ualberta.ca/folio/2020/01/millennials-and-gen-z-are-more-anxious-than-previous-generations-heres-why.html.

17. Romans 12:1–2 PHILLIPS.

18. See Spiritual Beings Series, BibleProject, https://bibleproject.com/explore/category/spiritual-beings-series/.

19. N. T. Wright, *Paul for Everyone: Romans, Part 1* (Louisville: Westminster John Knox, 2004), 75–76.

CHAPTER 9: FULL CIRCLE

1. Matthew 7:13–14.

2. Mark 10:17–31.

3. William Barclay, *Gospel of John*, vol. 1 (Philadelphia: Westminster, 1975), 128–29.
4. Mark 10:21.
5. Mark 10:22.
6. Mark 5:25–34.
7. Mark 10:27.